RINKs
Retired, Independent, No Kids

Retirement and Investment Advice For
People Without Children

by
Raymond D. Mignone, CFP®

Bloomington, IN  Milton Keynes, UK

authorHOUSE™

AuthorHouse™
1663 Liberty Drive, Suite 200
Bloomington, IN 47403
www.authorhouse.com
Phone: 1-800-839-8640

AuthorHouse™ UK Ltd.
500 Avebury Boulevard
Central Milton Keynes, MK9 2BE
www.authorhouse.co.uk
Phone: 08001974150

First published by AuthorHouse   6/14/2006

ISBN: 1-4259-3484-6 (sc)
ISBN: 1-4259-3483-8 (dj)
Printed in the United States of America
Bloomington, Indiana

This book is printed on acid-free paper.

Dedication

To my loving wife Paula. My partner in business and life. For
all of your patience and support.

Contents

Acknowledgements

A number of people have gone far beyond my expectations by reviewing and helping with this book. Special thanks to the RINKs who took the time to be reviewers; Edward Ciaccio, Elizabeth Bartle, Carol-Ann Brown, and Sylvia Morandina.

Thanks for the extra effort and time spent in reviewing, making corrections and suggestions in the legal areas; elder law attorney Vincent J. Russo, Esq. of the law firm of Vincent J. Russo & Associates and estate planning attorney Diane Wilke, Esq. of the law offices of Wilke & Wilke. Thanks also to Jed Albert, Esq. of the law firm of Farrell Fritz P.C.

To my fellow financial advisors and others who reviewed the different chapters and/or made some excellent suggestions including; Roz Liston, Andy Rich, Karen Altfest, Naomi Scrivener, Bob Kleinman, John Trotta, Nancy Frank, Tony Papa, Anthony DeVito, Chris Cooper and Walter Wisniewski.

Thanks to Steve Blank owner of the Times/Ledger newspapers and his great staff for giving me the opportunity to write my retirement and investment articles over the years.

Thanks for the long hours of tedious administrative support; Jesse Mignone, Natassia Palma and editing support by Kristi Mignone.

Many of the charts and projections in this book were produced using, Naviplan Extended Version 9g, by Emerging Information Systems Inc.

Very special thanks, to all of my clients, for trusting me with the management of their life savings, and allowing me to earn a living doing the work that I love.

Author's Note

Since becoming a CERTIFIED FINANCIAL PLANNER™ practitioner in 1989 I have helped many individuals and couples make a financially successful transition into retirement. Over the years, having created hundreds of retirement plans, I realized that a good portion of my clients, were like me, and don't have any children. Or, they can't count on children to assist with financial or emotional help during their golden years. Once retired, I respectfully refer to these clients as RINKs – Retired, Independent, No Kids.

I also realized that on average the clients without children, (who were savers), tended to have accumulated more assets during their lifetime than those clients with children. Their retirement, estate and health care planning needs are different, with our emphasis on ensuring independence and dignity in retirement.

Most importantly, the need to preserve and manage investments properly is critical to allowing them to enjoy a long and financially independent retirement. For these reasons our firm created a unique retirement planning and investment management process we call the, **RINKs Planning Strategy.**

As I searched for information to help my clients, I couldn't find any books specifically devoted to retirement and investment planning for childless individuals, who had accumulated some wealth. This gave me the motivation for writing RINKs. In this book, I share my years of experience working with individual retirees, making retirement projections, and managing their investments in a risk controlled manner. I describe the strategies and processes that we use with our clients, when implementing our unique, **RINKs Planning Strategy.**

The book covers many different aspects of personal finance, including some of the emotional issues of transitioning into retirement, and building a support network of advisors and friends. Of course no book can cover all aspects of personal wealth management. My hope is that this book will provide you with some ideas that you can utilize in your own life, or while working with your financial advisor.

Much of the information in the book will pertain to anyone whether they have children or not, but wherever possible I have explained why certain strategies are better for the childless. My hope is this book will help you optimize your wealth and happiness in retirement.

To make the book easier to read, rather than saying he/she every time I mention a professional advisor, I just use the male gender.

If you want more current information and articles on retirement and investment management, or to better understand our unique RINKs Planning Strategy, you can visit the RINKs area on our website: www.raymignone.com

1) RINKs
Retired, Independent, No Kids

Retirement at sixty-five is ridiculous.
When I was sixty-five I still had pimples.
                                                    -George Burns

You worked hard your entire life, sacrificing, saving, and now that you are in retirement you want to maintain your lifestyle, remain independent and live your life with dignity. These statements could be at the beginning of any retirement planning book. The difference is, like me, you don't have any children you can rely on in your golden years.

In your working years, you listened politely to cocktail party conversations about childrearing experiences and expenses. In retirement many of your friends will be spending time with their grandchildren, but not you. For many of my retired clients, visiting, babysitting or taking vacations with grandchildren occupies a large portion of their time. What will occupy your time in retirement? How will you pay for your retirement activities? Who will be there for you when you are ill?

Much of the current financial advice available doesn't apply to you. When saving for retirement, you don't need to understand college aide and tuition strategies. In retirement, you can ignore the conversations about using life insurance to preserve your estate for your children. You should be most concerned with having enough money to make sure you will be taken care of in your golden years.

If you are Retired, Independent, with No Kids, you are a RINK. My assumption is you have accumulated a sizable retirement nest egg, and now you need to insure that your wealth will work for you during your long retirement. Proper management of your wealth is important. It will enable you to pay for the additional services you will need in order to live out the rest of your life, independently and with dignity.

If you are childless, either as an individual or as a married couple, you face different retirement and health care planning issues than would someone with children. The key word in RINK is independent. In order to remain independent you need a certain amount of money. This book will try to help you manage your wealth more effectively, and to help you make intelligent life decisions in retirement.

As I defined it above, RINK stands for Retired, Independent, No Kids. What do you need to remain independent? I believe, a combination of a liquid net worth of at least $500,000 in addition to a home with no mortgage. If you don't have a monthly pension other then Social Security (and nowadays most people don't), you will need a much larger net worth or nest egg.

Of course it all depends on how much you spend and on your lifestyle. I will discuss this further in the chapters that follow on retirement planning. You will benefit from the ideas and strategies in this book if you don't have any children, but have at least $500,000 or more, saved for retirement.

Questions?

Some of the questions a RINK must consider are:

* Whom will you trust to watch and manage your money, as you get older?

* How do your take monthly distributions from your investments tax efficiently?

* How is your estate planning strategy different from that of someone with children?

* Who will take care of your pets if something happens to you?

* How do you go about making tax smart charitable donations?

* Who will be there to take care of you if you get ill?

* Who will monitor your doctors?

* Who will ensure your bills are paid if you need to be in the hospital short term?

* Can you count on family, nieces and nephews to be there for you in your time of need?

Throughout this book I will address these questions. In addition, I will present useful ideas and strategies so you can worry less and enjoy your retirement more.

The System Isn't Fair. Oh Well!

During your working years you paid more than your share of taxes and received less in services than people with children. As an individual, or married couple without children, you do not get all of the tax deductions that taxpayers with children get. Over the years, a lot of extra money was taken from your earnings that perhaps you would have otherwise saved. Now, in your retirement, this money is not available to you.

Will the federal government replace a child as your primary caregiver in your old age? No. Since you paid disproportionately more in income taxes, will the IRS call you each day to check if you are OK? Don't count on it. Will your local county or town credit your healthcare bills for all of the school taxes you paid? Not likely.

Some of my RINK friends complain that not only is the government taking more and giving them less, but so are their own families. Many grandparents will give more money each year to their children who bear them grandchildren. This takes the form of annual gifts and sometimes inheritances. Is this fair? I don't know; it's just the way it is. You need to accept it and do your own planning to insure independence in retirement. As a RINK, you have to be prepared to build your own support team and manage your affairs with your team.

Control Your Own Destiny

You are caught in the middle, not super rich but also not low income. This means you have to use your assets wisely and position yourself properly. Think about cultivating younger friends and relatives to support you through your golden years. When I ask my RINK friends what they have done to prepare for retirement without children, I receive blank stares. They haven't thought about it. They don't want to think about it. ***You must think about it!***

In order to control your destiny you need to have enough money. Your savings and investments are the cornerstone of your independence. To enable your money to last, it is important to make smart money decisions during your retirement. This will usually mean consulting with professionals along the way: financial advisors, elder law lawyers, and tax preparers.

You also need the help of an emotional support team. I will discuss both of your support teams, or what I refer to as your $Team and ETeam.

Establish An Experienced $Team

I believe every RINK needs to establish what I refer to as a money team, or *$Team*. This is a team you assemble over the years, to help you make better decisions with your money and your finances. This team could include many different players, but usually must include a trusted financial advisor as captain, an elder law/estate attorney and a tax preparer.

Getting good financial and legal advice will be invaluable to you as you progress into your golden years. Your wealth is the engine that generates the income needed throughout your retirement years. It needs to be managed properly. You should be getting the best advice you can from an experienced $Team you can trust.

Like a sports team, there is an owner and a captain. You are the owner of the $Team and make the final decisions. Your personal financial advisor should be the captain of your team. His job would be to coordinate all of the other $Team members that you will need, this will ensure a comprehensive approach in solving your financial issues. He should have the knowledge and experience to know when to bring in other professionals, and monitor their services for you.

If you don't already have a $Team, it is important to establish one early in retirement since you will need time to evaluate the trustworthiness of your advisors. You don't want to wait until you are in your late 70s to put together a $Team. This may not allow enough time to establish a loyal, trusting relationship.

Trust and loyalty is a two way street. Think about any business relationship you have had in your lifetime. It takes time to establish loyalty and trust. Have you ever had a client or customer that was always shopping around looking for the lowest price, or perhaps only gave you part of his business, or called you sporadically just to pick your brain? Would you have loyalty to that client? Would you drop everything you were doing in order to help that client if he called with an emergency?

As a RINK when you get older, you will need to have a team of professionals who are already familiar with your situation. More importantly, you will need a team that will go the extra mile for you when you need it most, perhaps when you are not physically or mentally able to make good decisions on your own. You will need professionals you can rely on to make objective decisions, in your best interests during a personal crisis, such as the death of a spouse, relative or close friend.

With a good solid $Team you can spend your retirement enjoying life more and worrying about financial issues less. In another chapter I will discuss in great detail how to select a trusted financial advisor. You may decide to manage your affairs on your own as long as you can. In that case, I believe the information presented in this book will also be very helpful to you.

Establish An ETeam

ETeam is my term, for your Emotional Support Team. This team is not as clearly defined as the $Team, but it's just as important and I will try to explain what I mean. Mostly, your ETeam will include a reliable support network of friends and relatives who are young enough to be able to help and comfort you, in retirement. The captain of this team may end up being a competent, caring Geriatric Care Manager if no family member is available.

You need to ask yourself:

Who will monitor my doctors?

Who will ask the right medical questions for me?

Who will listen to my fears?

Who will talk with me to keep me engaged in the world?

Who will check to see that I am all right?

Who will check to see that I'm not left lying on the floor for 3 days, alone?

My wife calls her 87-year-old mother everyday to see how she is doing. Who will call you? Even if you are a married RINK, at some point you will end up living on your own. Not a pleasant thought, yet unfortunately part of your destiny.

Your ETeam will include both professionals and personal relationships, which you purposely establish. The professionals will include of course your doctors, but with the way the medical system is today, it is difficult for a doctor to spend much time with you. If you don't have a close relative or friend, the captain of this team may end up being a competent, caring Geriatric Care Manager.

With enough money, you can purchase many services, and that is why it is so important for you to manage your wealth properly. A geriatric care manager is a professional who has knowledge of many aging issues and can assist you with a variety of problems. They can coordinate many of your needs, including nurses, transportation, bill paying and coordination with other elder care professionals. I will discuss geriatric care managers in more detail in the chapter on Health Care and Incapacity Planning.

Hopefully, your ETeam will include a reliable network of caring friends and relatives who are young enough to be able to help you when you need assistance. You may have a family member who can be the captain of your ETeam. However, many RINKs can't count on that.

You will likely find other RINKs in the same situation as yourself. You can create your own informal network of friends who will support each other in times of need. One of my clients has an informal arrangement with her neighbor. Each day, if her window shade isn't pulled up by a certain time, that's the signal something is wrong. Not very high tech, but it works! You can come up with your own system. The point is you must be sure someone is watching out for you.

Having Enough Wealth Is Important

I don't think most people realize how much money will be required to maintain their current lifestyle throughout a long

30+ year retirement. Entering retirement with a large net worth is an important first step. Properly investing and managing your money in a tax efficient manner, during a long retirement, is the cornerstone of a successful retirement.

You arrive at this stage of your life due to hard work, sacrifice and saving. It is important for your continued financial success to plan intelligently, avoid major mistakes and implement strategies that are relevant to you as a RINK.

Chapter Summary

My definition of a RINK is someone who is Retired, Independent, with No Kids. By financially independent, I mean owning your home free and clear with at least $500,000 in a retirement nest egg.

You should establish an experienced $Team. The captain should be a trusted financial advisor and the team members should be other professionals such as an elder law attorney and tax preparer. This team could make or break your financial success in retirement.

You should also establish an ETeam or emotional team. The ETeam will consist of a network of friends and/or family members who will assist you as you age. The team captain may be a paid, caring geriatric care manager, if no friend or relative is available.

Having enough money to pay for extra services is the cornerstone of a long successful retirement.

2) Preparation For Retirement

The beginning is the most important part of the work.
                                                    -Plato

If you are to have a financially successful retirement as a RINK your planning has to start many years in advance of your chosen retirement date. It starts by saving and investing for the future while you are young and while others with children are spending their money away on sweet sixteen parties, weddings and education expenses.

The good news is that people without children are in the position to save a lot more money during their working years. I don't have scientific statistics but after meeting with many clients and prospective clients over the years, with all other things being equal, (earnings, age, saving discipline, etc.), savers without children amass a significant amount more in assets than savers with children.

Now, you might disagree because as a RINK, you pay a lot more in income taxes over your lifetime. You don't get the tax deductions and credits that are given when you have children but the expenses of raising children add up to far more than the additional taxes you may have paid.

What is saving anyway? Well, simply it is the restraining of immediate consumption for the benefit of delayed gratification. The delayed gratification you want to achieve is a financially secure retirement so that you can remain independent, maintain your desired lifestyle, and have enough money to provide for services that someone who has children might otherwise get help with from their children. My intention in this book is not to teach you how to save for retirement. This book is written for someone either in retirement or near retirement without children who has already amassed a significant retirement nest egg. Having said that, I think it is important to understand how regular savings and investing can add up.

Regular Investments

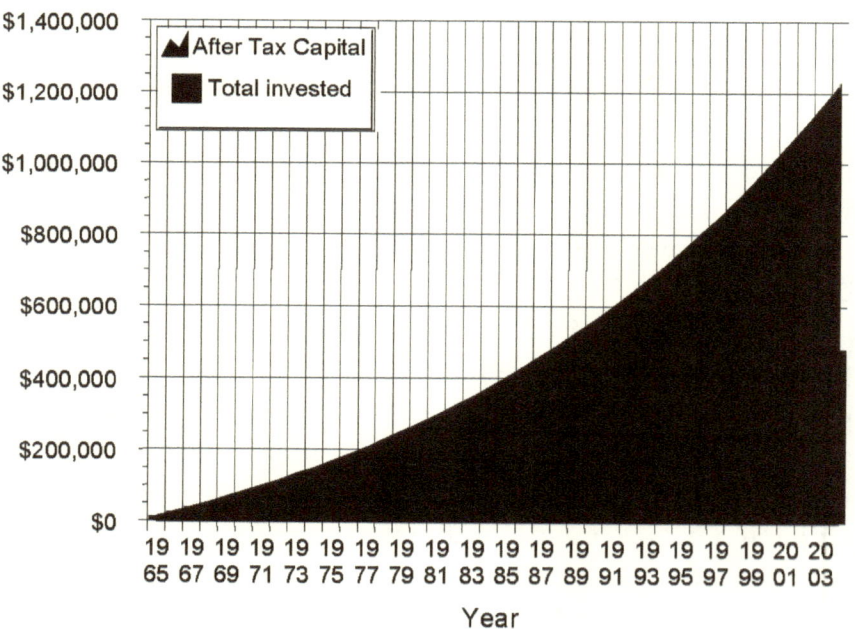

Figure 1

I have included a graph (Figure 1) to help you visualize the effects of regular savings. The graph shows that if you started investing at age 20 in 1965 with $1,000 initially, and adding $1,000 each month over 40 years with a 6% taxable return and paying an average 30% in taxes each year, you would accumulate just over $1,200,000 by the time you reach age 60.

Past Planning Enables Today's Harvest

When I was a young boy growing up in the Richmond Hill section of Queens, N.Y., my father always had a large vegetable garden. He had five children to feed and since he was raised on a small farm in Southern Italy he knew how to manage our little city garden. In the fall he would have my brother and I, rake all of the leaves into his garden and then proceed to bury them in the dirt. While we were burying our leaves my neighbor Louie would be burning his in a 50-gallon drum, which, to me, seemed like a much faster way to complete the job.

When I questioned my father about this and why we didn't burn our leaves since it was faster, he smiled and said, "We are planning now for next summer's bountiful harvest." Frankly it wasn't until years later that I understood how my father's composting turned the dirt into black gold and that is why he always had the best vegetable garden in the neighborhood.

I share this story because it explains what I have witnessed while creating many retirement plans for clients. Those who arrive at their retirement with sizable wealth planned and saved years ahead preparing for their future harvest. They arrive in many cases with their home mortgage-free, no debt and with $500,000 or more in investment assets.

Do I consider these people rich? Maybe the rich people are the ones who are healthy, happy and content with their current lifestyle. I can't put a dollar value on that. From my experience, these folks are middle class people who have positioned themselves so that with proper money management they can enjoy their lifestyle during their 30+ years of retirement and not have to worry about money. The key at this point in your life is how to make the smartest money decisions from now on. I will try to explain this in detail in the following chapters.

RINKs Need A Larger Nest Egg

I am going to repeat this many times in this book, since I can't stress enough how important this is: **As a RINK you need to have more money in your retirement nest egg than someone who has children on whom they can rely.** This is not so evident when you first retire and you are healthy, say in your 60's or early 70's, but as you get older, you will need more help and services. It is at this point in your life when you will be most vulnerable since you can't just call up a son or daughter to come over to help you or to pick up your groceries.

At that point in your life you might have to consider hiring a geriatric care manager to assist you. I will talk about them later in the chapter on health care and incapacity planning. You will have to pay for these additional expenses and services when you are not in a position to increase your earnings. As a RINK, you need a much larger buffer of additional net wealth to allow for these additional services.

Retirement Psychology

One of the most important preparations for retirement has less to do with money and everything to do with psychology. The people who are happiest in retirement are those who have hobbies, interests or social organizations to keep them busy. They also don't spend their valuable time worrying about their day-to-day investment results. Have I hired outside consultants to do an elaborate study to prove my point? No! Here is how I formulate my theory. I just pick up the phone and call one of my retired clients to make an appointment to come in for a review meeting.

But they are often not home, or not available to come in for weeks. Why? Because they are too busy. Retired and too busy!

What are these people doing? Ok, sure some are golfing. But Pat and Helen are either in Atlantic City or visiting friends. Liz is going to see another Broadway show with her retired teacher friends. (I think she has seen every show on Broadway). If I try to reach Andy, he is out working in his large yard because the gardener just doesn't get things right. Frank and Rosemary are always traveling to some sunny climate. If you think you will not be active when you are in the late stages of retirement, think again. When I call Hella and she is not home, it's either because she is taking the subway to Manhattan to her weekly art class or she's going to the opera. Hella is 92! Doris is out volunteering at the hospital, helping "the old infirm people." Doris is 91!

I believe it is very important for you, as a RINK, to be involved with many activities, clubs and social organizations. This will keep your mind busy and off your aches and pains. In addition it will help you build a solid network of friends that could possibly be there to assist you when you need some additional support.

Of course, it's always best to get involved with organizations that you have a strong interest in, but your involvement with religious or charitable organizations may help you establish strong friendships with people who are already predisposed to being sympathetic and caring. These people should form the core of your Emotional Support Team (ETeam). You will likely find other RINKs and you can create your own informal network of friends who will be there to support one another in times of need.

Are You Mentally Prepared?

The most important preparation for retirement is getting yourself mentally prepared to fill your previous working hours with other activities. Some folks have a difficult time making the transition. I have done several retirement plans for clients who were planning on retiring within a few years, but they didn't retire.

We go over the entire process, and evaluate their cash flow needs, considering inflation, taxes and increased spending. We review all of their income, reposition the investment portfolio, and everything looks great. I even run a Monte Carlo (a form of probability analysis) report against their retirement plan to insure the probability that the investments will last during their lifetimes in various market conditions. After everything looks positive for a successful retirement, and they don't retire!

Why, I ask? Here are some responses:

"If I work another year I'll get more benefits" (this is a good one, since clients know financial planners like to see more pension income in retirement).

"The firm needs time to train someone to replace me" (hey a good boss knows how to stroke your ego).

"My friend retired and within a year he was dead" (would you prefer to die on your desk at work?).

The truth is more along the lines of fear of change. For someone who has gone from high school to the military and/or to college to 40 years in a working career, not having to be somewhere everyday is scary. Many people, frankly, are worried about being home alone or alone with their spouse 24 hours a day. There is that old joke: "I married for better or worst, but not for lunch."

I think that the primary reason some folks don't retire when they could has more to do with self-esteem. Let's face it, at the office you are important and people value your opinions, skills, and experience. At this stage of your career you are most likely the well-respected, wise sage of the office. If you had your own business you are used to telling people what to do, and, yes, they listen, (or have no job). When you retire, try bossing your spouse around all day! Well, maybe the dog will listen (sometimes). You need a reason to get up each morning.

Afraid To Stop Saving?

Another of the major barriers to actually retiring is the idea of not continuing to save money. This may sound crazy, but you should see the look on people's faces when I show them the monthly dollar withdrawals from their retirement portfolio that is needed each month to sustain their current lifestyle in retirement (never mind that the withdrawals may be only a small part of their investment return).

Here it is you did an excellent job of working hard, sacrificing, and saving your entire life, and now you are faced with the reality that you will no longer be saving and, in most cases, you will be withdrawing from your nest egg in order to live. You have to get comfortable with this new idea. Having someone competent develop a retirement plan with you may increase your comfort level and confidence that you will not run out of money.

To help you understand how your money can be drawn down each year I have included The Payout Duration from Investments chart (Figure 2). This gives you an idea of what would happen if you started with $500,000 and withdrew $50,000 each year after taxes assuming you made 6% taxable interest on your money and paid taxes at an average rate of 30%. You can see from the chart that you would run out of money by age 78, not a successful strategy. (Inflation was not taken into consideration or you would have run out of money sooner, as you will see in the next chapter)

When Should You Retire?

At what point do you actually make that scary decision to retire? In order to make an intelligent decision, you really need to perform a thorough cash flow and budget analysis, review your pension options, and, only then, will you be in a position to make an intelligent decision.

Payout Duration from Investments

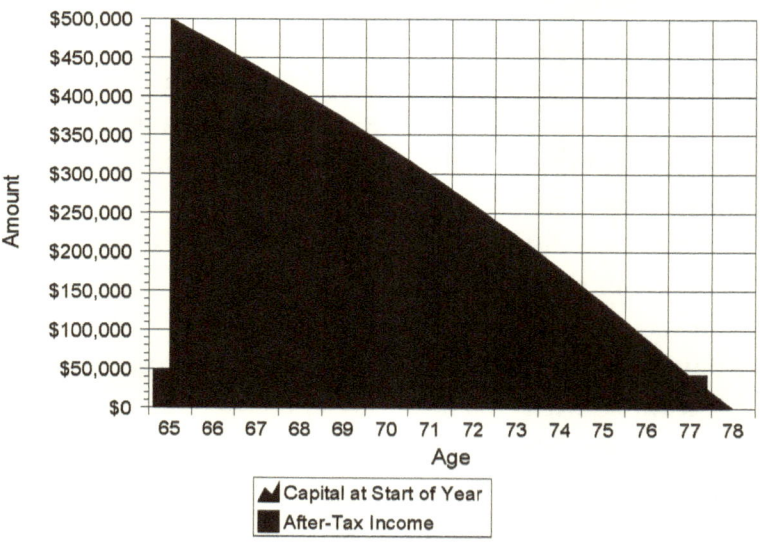

Year	Age	Market Value	After-Tax Monthly Indexed Payout
2005	65	500,000	4,167
2006	66	469,877	4,167
2007	67	438,488	4,167
2008	68	405,782	4,167
2009	69	371,701	4,167
2010	70	336,190	4,167
2011	71	299,186	4,167
2012	72	260,629	4,167
2013	73	220,452	4,167
2014	74	178,588	4,167
2015	75	134,966	4,167
2016	76	89,511	4,167
2017	77	42,147	3,569
2018	78	0	0

Figure 2

Many RINKs love their work and have no intention of ever retiring. They like the money coming in and the involvement of the work environment. Others decide to stay on the job longer to create that extra buffer in savings that the RINK will need later in retirement. Delaying retirement will create a larger nest egg, since you will be saving for a few more years and you will delay your portfolio withdrawals. These combined actions may make the difference in having a financially successful retirement.

More and more people are moving from full time work to part time if their company allows this. I see business professionals reduce their workloads so they can work three days a week and still make good money. This is an ideal way to ease into retirement while continuing to earn money. A good retirement analysis is the best way to determine when you can retire or how much you need to earn if you retired early but worked part time. In the next chapter we will look at the retirement planning process in more detail to better enable you to make these important decisions.

Chapter Summary

You worked hard all of your life, you sacrificed and saved so you would arrive at retirement with significant investments. You will need a larger retirement nest egg than people with children, since you will likely need to pay for additional services when you get older. You also have to get yourself mentally prepared to leave the work environment. Many people have a hard time doing this, since they are afraid they will be unimportant once retired.

You have to get comfortable with the idea that you are now starting to reverse the process with your money: in your working years, you earned and saved: now you will be drawing down your investments to support your lifestyle. As many others are doing, you should consider working part time for a few years so you can adjust to a full time retirement. The objective is for your money to last as long as your life.

3) Pre-retirement Planning

We Plan and God Laughs.
-Unknown

Your individual circumstances will determine when it would be best for you to retire. I cannot stress enough how important it is to review your own personal financial situation and not listen to the advice given at the office water cooler. As a prospective RINK you have to be a little more cautious in deciding when to retire, especially if you are not married at the time of your retirement decision. A married couple usually has more sources of income and a greater net worth than a single individual.

How is your health? Your health may play a large role in your retirement decision, especially if you will not be receiving medical benefits in retirement and are too young to receive Medicare health benefits. If you have a preexisting condition you must be sure you can get and keep health coverage until Medicare begins.

Can you start collecting Social Security immediately? Social Security benefits are still a large portion of some retirees' income stream and if you will not be collecting Social Security immediately, you will have to have increased withdrawals from your portfolio to make up the difference until you will be eligible to collect Social Security.

Do you have a pension? If you have a defined benefit pension you are one of the lucky ones, since most companies have done away with these plans. Of course a sizeable monthly pension check in addition to Social Security helps make the retirement decision easier. I think you start to get the picture of what needs to be considered, so let's cover some of the issues.

Pre-Retirement VS Retirement Planning

If you have not yet retired, you need what is called a *pre-retirement planning review* in order to tell you how much you need to save for retirement or how much longer you should wait to retire. There is really not much difference between pre-retirement planning and ongoing planning while in retirement. Pre-retirement planning is usually done to help you make the decision *when* you should retire, typically around age 55. It is valuable in helping you select which pension option you should be taking and determining how you will fund those extra expenses if you retire early and have delayed benefits. If you retire early you may not be eligible for social security yet, and you may need to purchase temporary health care coverage prior to Medicare starting at age 65.

If you are already retired, then you should do a postretirement plan to evaluate your current financial situation, including reviewing your current expenses, taxes, income stream, and the ability of your investment portfolio to continue to provide your support. You should review what has changed since you retired, and what needs to be adjusted now, before it is too late.

In order to decide if you can afford to retire, maintain your lifestyle and your dignity during the remainder of your lifetime, you need to do a complete retirement analysis. I don't see how you can make one of the most important decisions in your life without gathering all of the facts for an objective analysis. Most people spend more time researching a vacation than doing a good job of planning for their retirement.

Of course you will say I am biased since I am a financial planner, but I believe planning really pays for itself. A CERTIFIED FINANCIAL PLANNER™ professional can help you create an objective retirement plan prior to your deciding to retire. This is usually most beneficial a few years prior to retirement, or just before you have to make some major financial decisions. In another chapter I will give you tips on how to find a good financial advisor who is also a financial planner. I will cover pre-retirement planning and post-retirement planning as one process, since most of the issues are the same.

Should You Do Your Own Planning?

This is what most people have done for years by default: They talk to friends and relatives, look at their pension options and current expenses, estimate a return on their investments, and make a decision. Sometimes they will attend a company-sponsored retirement seminar with a room full of other potential retirees. Unfortunately, in many cases this can lead to bad decisions that don't show up until you realize you are beginning to run out of money many years later and are not in a position to go back to work. Remember: your goal as a RINK is to never end up in this position.

If you are good with numbers and analytical, there is plenty of retirement planning software available for consumers. Using one or more of these planning tools will be a significant help to you. If you look on the Web you will find every discount broker, financial website and financial magazine website offering free planning tools. Some of these are very good but extremely limited, and some are outright terrible and will produce misleading results. The biggest problems with most of these planning methods are oversimplification and optimistic assumptions. The planning

Payout Duration from Investments

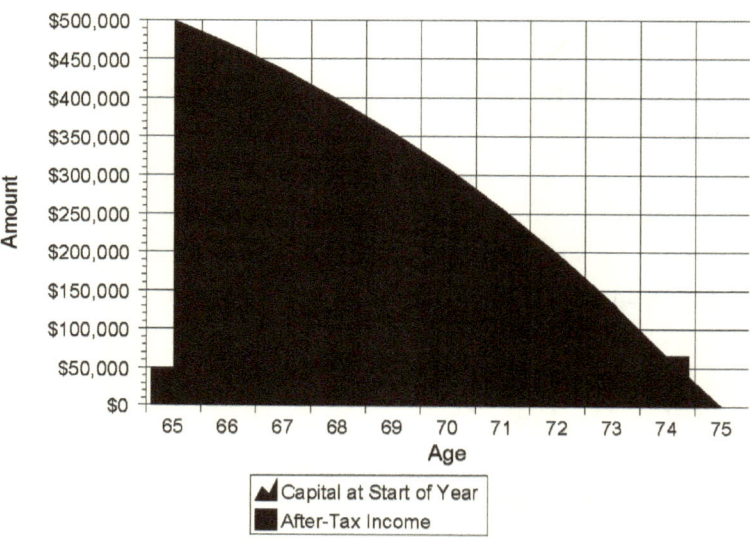

Year	Age	Market Value	After-Tax Monthly Indexed Payout
2005	65	500,000	4,167
2006	66	469,877	4,375
2007	67	435,932	4,594
2008	68	397,878	4,823
2009	69	355,407	5,065
2010	70	308,194	5,318
2011	71	255,891	5,584
2012	72	198,128	5,863
2013	73	134,514	6,156
2014	74	64,631	5,472
2015	75	0	0

Figure 3

tools that are the quickest, ask fewer questions and will provide the poorest results.

Some of the other problems with inexpensive retirement planning software is the inability to correctly model your taxes. Including the effect of your state income tax, the taxation of your pension and the significant effects of how your tax bracket increases when you must start taking your Required Minimum Distributions at age 70 ½.

All financial planning modeling involves making projections based on assumptions from current information both unique to you and assumptions on future taxes, inflation rates and investment returns. While the calculator you use may be extremely accurate based on the data you enter, how valid are your assumptions? Remember, as with all computer software, if you put garbage information in, you will get garbage out.

To give you an idea of how different assumptions could drastically change the outcome see Payout Duration From Investments (Figure 3), in which I added a 5% inflation rate that was not included in Figure 2. Note you would run out of money about 3 years earlier simply due to the inflation rate being added to the projections.

Have Someone Review Your Information

In my financial planning and investment management firm I specialize in working with retirees and people transitioning into retirement. Over the years I have done many retirement plans for clients. There are some people who are extremely analytical and come to my office with their Quicken or Excel spreadsheets in hand and really believe they have accounted for every expense and they just want to get an objective second opinion. During the data gathering part of the process we find out that major expenses were left out.

Even these very analytical individuals who can account for every expense leave out some large recurring expenses such as automobile purchases. When I ask where are the car purchase costs, the reply is usually "we always buy our cars outright". This is great and I recommend it for most folks in retirement but you need to ask:

If you paid $40,000 for that Lexus, where did the money come from?
In how many years will you be replacing it?
How much will that Lexus cost in 8 years at 4% inflation?
How do you account for that in your software, since you will be selling assets to purchase many vehicles over your retirement?
How do you offset the taxes generated by the sale of assets to fund the vehicle?
These are all things you need to take into consideration.

Some of the biggest errors I see come from the client not having experience in considering certain expenses or scenarios. So I would recommend that before you start making decisions based on the output of data from a financial planning software program it would be a good idea to read several of the very fine retirement planning books which are available. This will help you consider many of the details that you should be putting into your data and should help you make better decisions.

Can You Be Objective?

Another problem with making retirement decisions based on doing your own retirement planning is the ability to look at your own financial situation in an objective manner. Most people just cannot do it.

The topic is filled with emotionally-charged decisions such as:
Do I need to scale back my lifestyle?
Will I sell the large house I lived in for 30 years to move into a smaller less expensive home?

Should I move away from my family and friends on Long Island to live in Florida, to save on property and income tax? Can I still afford the second home in the country even though no one ever wants to go there anymore?

Sometimes, especially between husband and wife (and especially if this is a second marriage), issues come up in a retirement planning meeting that the couple has never discussed before, or they have been avoiding discussing for years. A good example is that, typically, a RINK couple does not want to contemplate the eventual and inevitable loss of their spouse.

A good financial planner has to be able to read the emotions and body language of the clients in order to help them determine what is really important since many retirement decisions will require changes in lifestyle. At times, the financial planner has to be part counselor and part psychologist in order to get agreement on what is important.

In pre-retirement planning, one of the most important and emotionally-charged decisions is whether to select the single-life, 50% survivor, or some other option on the pension payout of one spouse. Most times one spouse is dominant and may push a choice with which the other spouse is uncomfortable. If you decide to make your retirement decision based on your own planning, I suggest you have a friend or family member you feel has good common sense at least review your assumptions. Perhaps he/she will see something you missed.

Effects Of Inflation

The enemy of retirees is inflation. Since RINKs will likely require more services than others in retirement, inflation on services (which has risen more than regular inflation) presents a big challenge. I have included two charts (Figure 4) to give you an idea of the impact of inflation on your cost of living because I don't think most people fully realize how important inflation is in making retirement decisions.

Impact of Inflation on the Cost of Living

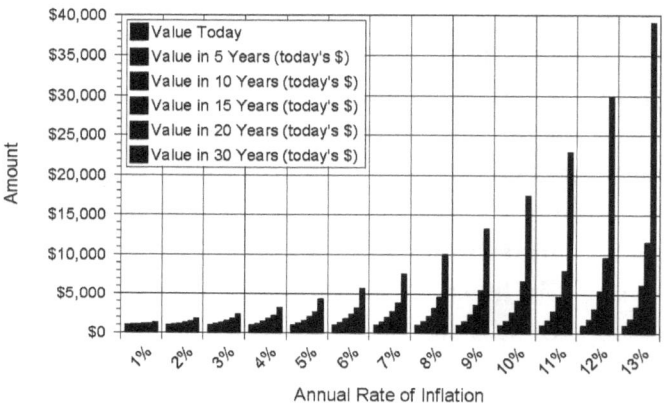

Annual Rate of Inflation	Value Today	Value in 5 Years (today's $)	Value in 10 Years (today's $)	Value in 20 Years (today's $)	Value in 30 Years (today's $)
1.00%	1,000	1,051	1,105	1,220	1,348
2.00%	1,000	1,104	1,219	1,486	1,811
3.00%	1,000	1,159	1,344	1,806	2,427
4.00%	1,000	1,217	1,480	2,191	3,243
5.00%	1,000	1,276	1,629	2,653	4,322
6.00%	1,000	1,338	1,791	3,207	5,743
7.00%	1,000	1,403	1,967	3,870	7,612
8.00%	1,000	1,469	2,159	4,661	10,063
9.00%	1,000	1,539	2,367	5,604	13,268
10.00%	1,000	1,611	2,594	6,727	17,449
11.00%	1,000	1,685	2,839	8,062	22,892
12.00%	1,000	1,762	3,106	9,646	29,960
13.00%	1,000	1,842	3,395	11,523	39,116

Figure 4

If you choose an annual rate of inflation on the bottom left of the chart you can view how much money you will need in the future to buy the same amount of goods and services that would cost you $1,000 today. For example, if your monthly expenses today are $10,000 a month and inflation is 5% and you want to know how much you will need in 20 years if you maintain the same standard of living.

Using the table, find the 5% inflation rate row on the left for $1,000. Move over to the right column and find the number under the "Value in 20 Years" column, look down to where it intersects the 5% row and you see $2,653. If you spend $10,000 a month today, ($2,653 x 10 = $26,530). In 20 years you will need to spend $26,530 a month to essentially buy the same goods and services you get today with just $10,000.

The Retirement Planning Process

I want to discuss many important retirement planning topics in detail and I would like to do this by taking you through a typical retirement planning process throughout the rest of this chapter and the next chapter. Whether you decide to work with a financial planner or plan for your own retirement this will give you one way to approach the process.

Of course, each planner has his own retirement planning process using different financial planning software and asking different questions. Some may have a very structured process and others may have a more casual, friendly style. Just as with any other professional his work style will reflect his personality. However, no matter how his methods may vary a good planner will cover all of your important issues. If you are doing the planning for yourself, you will notice that different questions are asked of you, depending on the author who wrote the planning self-help book you may be reading.

I will discuss the way I typically approach the planning process in my practice with my clients and, hopefully this will help you get an idea of what you should be looking for. Of course, I can't cover all the issues that may come up in a planning engagement because every client has their own individual personal needs and issues.

The planning may drift off into different directions depending on what is important to you. For example, after reviewing charitable deductions on your tax return, if you were charitably-inclined the planner would discuss all of the available options for gifting in the most tax-efficient way.

Someone else with similar assets and minimum charitable deductions on their tax return may say, "Hey, I worked hard all my life and no one ever gave me anything so I'm holding on to my money till I die." With this person I wouldn't spend much time discussing charitable giving. In any case, I think you can see why the planning process needs to be adapted to your own unique financial situation.

What Prompted The Planning Process?

Usually there is one major reason or question that must be answered to prompt someone to visit a financial planner. For example someone who will possibly be retiring in six months may need to make decisions such as which pension options should be taken or what should be done with the 401k money. Typically, to answer these questions properly requires a thorough analysis of the family's financial situation. Some people may want to shortcut the analysis process and just give you a quick "from my experience," off-the-cuff answer, but in order to make a truly informed decision, I don't see how you can do it without performing a detailed analysis.

Many issues are interrelated. For example, if you take the payout annuity option from your retirement plan, you may not have to worry about investing that money, but the income tax and estate tax repercussions are different than if you roll over the money into an IRA and use other after-tax money for living expenses. You can't visualize this properly unless all of the information that describes your personal circumstances is put into a sophisticated cash-flow financial planning software program that has your current tax tables built into it. Then you need to model both scenario options and compare them. Only after that, can you make your best-informed "guess" of which is the right decision for you.

Chapter Summary

In this chapter I discussed that the Pre-retirement planning occurs prior to retirement and usually helps determine when you should retire and what pension options you should choose. Post-retirement planning is general financial planning that should continue to monitor your financial life all during retirement.

Should you attempt to do your own retirement planning or hire a CERTIFIED FINANCIAL PLANNER™ professional? When doing your own planning you can get assistance from the Internet and retirement planning books and you should have someone review your work prior to making decisions. However, in doing your own planning, you lose the objectivity and wisdom of a professional who has much experience doing what you are attempting to do on your own. He also will have access to much more sophisticated financial planning software.

We covered the effects inflation has on a long retirement plan and that inflation is enemy #1 of the retiree. There is usually some initial decision that has to be made which will prompt someone to start thinking of doing retirement planning. It is best to do a complete financial analysis in order to make important decisions.

In an effort to help you understand some aspects of retirement you should be concerned with when doing planning, in the next chapter I will take you through a typical retirement planning engagement I follow with my new clients.

4) Retirement Planning Process

If you don't know where you are going, you'll end up somewhere else.

-Yogi Berra

Planning Initial Meeting

Let's get started with retirement planning. Please remember I am explaining the process that I use in my firm with a new client in order for you to better understand how the planning process works. The first communication from a new client usually begins with a phone conversation during which you (the client) explain your situation to the planner and the planner assesses if he is the appropriate person to take on the planning project for you.

Your assessment of the planner should be whether he has the expertise to handle your particular situation. For example, if you have issues that involve international taxes be sure the planner has experience in that area. Once you decide that there is a good fit set an initial appointment. My typical retirement planning analysis will take place over two to three meetings with most of the analysis work done between meetings.

What To Bring To The First Meeting

You should bring copies of most of your financial records to the first meeting. These include: latest tax returns, copies of insurance policies, wills, health care proxy, durable power of attorney, pay stubs, 401k/457/403b company statements, the latest brokerage, bank or other financial statements, latest mortgage statement or outstanding loan statements and anything else you might feel is important.

You should specifically bring your latest benefits information from the department of Social Security as well as the latest statements of your company's pension benefits and stock options if you are still working. Bring whatever other documents you believe might be helpful.

Some people are fearful of showing the planner "all of their personal business" before working with him. You should bring everything and leave it in your briefcase. If you are comfortable with the planner, then you will share the information; if not, then you will take the information back home. I had one client who, at our first meeting, carried in two milk crates with all of his files just in case we might need something! I don't recommend going that far, but please don't come to the first meeting empty handed. By doing this, you are wasting everyone's time and the planner won't take you seriously.

You are not there to just have a chat. In order for the planner to help you he must see certain pieces of your financial life and as long as what you show the planner is not copied and you take it back home, you have nothing to lose by showing it to him (unless you think he has a photographic memory).

The Planner Needs To Understand You

It is important for the planner to spend time listening to your particular situation and finding out what is important to you prior to jumping in to work on the details. Many clients want to rush into the details, but the planner can look over the financial details after you leave. What he needs to understand is how you want to live your life in retirement and what the major questions are you want answered in order to better enable you to make good

BUDGET/CASH FLOW DETAILS FOR Jones

CATEGORY	MONTHLY EXPENSE	YEARLY EXPENSE	COMMENTS
ELECTRIC	241	2892	
HEAT	139	1668	
WATER	40	480	
PHONE(ALL)	205	2460	
INTERNET SERVICE	75	900	
CABLE T-V	0	0	
VEHICLE PAYMENTS	0	0	
VEHICLE INS. (ALL)	200	2400	
FUEL/VEHICLES	225	2700	
TOLLS	0	0	
CAR REPAIRS	100	1200	
CAR REGISTRATION	8	100	
LIFE INSURANCE	0	0	
HEALTH INS.	917	11004	
OTHER INS.	0	0	
DENTAL	167	2000	
MEDICAL SUPPLIES	0	0	
DOCTOR BILLS/CO-PAY	80	960	
HAIRCUTS	25	300	
FOOD	1600	19200	
ENTERTAINMENT	200	2400	
EATING OUT	500	6000	
BIRTHDAY GIFTS	100	1200	
HOLIDAY GIFTS	150	1800	
CLOTHES	100	1200	
HOME INS.	75	900	
HOME REPAIRS	100	1200	
HOME IMPROVEMENT	0	0	
GARDENER	150	1800	
HOUSE CLEANING	300	3600	
SERVICE CONTRACTS	0	0	
VACATION	208	2500	
DAYCARE/BABY SITTERS	0	0	
MISC CHARITY	150	1800	
TAX PREPARATION FEE	42	500	
CREDIT CARD BILL	0	0	
MISC. (PLEASE EXPLAIN}	0	0	
MISC. (PLEASE EXPLAIN}	0	0	
MONTHLY SUB TOTAL	$6,097	$73,164	
YEARLY TOTAL	$73,164		

Figure 5

33

decisions. This usually requires a 30-minute interview process, so please try and relax. This is your financial planner's office not your dentist's office. We try to make clients feel comfortable by offering them cookies and a cappuccino during this time.

You may wonder, "Why is it important for the planner to know so much about my personal life when all I want him to do is tell me how to make good decisions with my money?" The end result is good advice on money decisions, but the goal is the best possible decisions on how to use your money to allow you to enjoy your retirement and the rest of your life. In order to do that properly, the planner requires a solid understanding of your personal situation because these facts might affect the recommendations given to you. The fact that you don't have children is very important for the planner to know since it opens up different planning strategies than for instance, someone with a disabled adult child.

For example you may be 62, retiring and you have helped put your niece through college. Now you may have to help support your mother who is 85 or your sister who is recently divorced with young children. You have to determine whether you can still afford these bills when you retire. Or perhaps you feel it is important for you to leave a large legacy to your nieces and nephews once you are gone so their lives are made easier.

Your number one priority is having enough money during retirement to be able to live your desired lifestyle with dignity and independence. If these other issues will put your retirement in jeopardy, then the planner must show you with numbers what your trade-off will be and perhaps just flat out tell you that you need to take care of yourself first.

It is important to understand family matters in order to make good financial decisions and for the planner to be able to give you good advice. If you could care less about leaving any money to your family, then the advice would certainly be different. If you are single, have no children and no one is relying on you for support then why are you still paying large annual premiums on that life insurance policy you were sold years ago? Maybe you need to review the necessity of this policy.

With all of these issues covered, you define the scope of the retirement planning analysis. The planner understands what is important to you by developing your short and long-term goals. You are typically given a Fact Finder questionnaire, which asks for even more details and information to complete and return to the planner.

Data Input and Initial Analysis

The Fact Finder or data gatherer is a form that pulls together all of your financial information in one place in the order that the planning software requires it. Once the planner receives all of the data from you, a para-planner usually reviews it and requests a list of missing information. Many times as the process is started, you will be asked to clarify certain situations because they may not be clear. Usually any additional information can be provided via email or with a phone call. While a complete Fact Finder form would take up too many pages, I have included a sample (Figure 5, information gatherer budget sheet) that we use to help define your current spending.

The planner will input the data and will begin to model or analyze your current situation. Some initial research may need to be done if your situation is complex. For example, if you have a complex stock option situation that has to be understood especially the tax consequences of handling your company stock options. Once all of the information has been gathered and the planner has been able to define your goals and understand your concerns, then the second meeting is set up.

The "Working" Second Planning Meeting

Here is where I believe interactive planning differs from most basic financial planning. Most planners gather the data from the first meeting, define the objectives, do the analysis and produce a written report. Then you come in for a second and final visit. Typically the output of the report is explained to you and the retirement planning is complete. Most people go home with charts, graphs and rows of numbers.

They either don't understand or don't have any confidence in the projections because they didn't participate in the development of the plan. In many cases the projections contain errors that are not caught and you are making important decisions based on poor or incorrect data.

Please understand that at many firms, especially the large brokerage firms, financial planning is used just to get you to the next step, which is purchasing investment or insurance products because the money is made on the products and not on the planning. Typically, the person presenting the "plan book" of reports to you may not have done the analysis. It was sent out to a staff person to complete. Therefore the advisor may not really understand all of the issues involved in the development of your plan.

Interactive Planning Ensures Good Results

In our second meeting, I usually spend about two hours with the client verifying that the assumptions of the plan are correct, reviewing the details and explaining how the projections are produced. I walk the client through the data on a large computer monitor that everyone can view at the same time. In 100% of the cases we find errors or you may want to change some of the assumptions. You may want to use a higher inflation rate or a lower rate of return on investments to make the plan more conservative. Maybe the expenses on the summer house look too high or the need to make health insurance payments before age 65 was never addressed when you submitted the Fact Finder. This meeting provides an opportunity to correct errors, change assumptions, add additional vacation spending and immediately see the financial results.

Next, I explain your annual cash flow projections by stepping quickly through each year, showing how much taxes are paid, how your expenses are increasing with inflation, and how your portfolio is generating taxable interest, dividends and long term gains each year. It is amazing to most people when they see how their taxable income jumps when they must start taking required minimum distributions at age 70 ½ from their IRAs and retirement plans. In many cases retired professionals such as medical practitioners have sheltered significant sums of money into their retirement plans and don't truly understand how much will be lost to income taxes when they are forced to withdraw at age 70 ½.

I have included a chart, (Figure 6, Projected Cash Flow Details) to give you an idea of the summary of a few years of cash flow projections. The top section shows the summaries by major categories of your cash flow coming into your household and the bottom shows all of the cash flows going out each year. Depending on how much detail the client likes to see, I can also show a very detailed breakdown of all projections.

Projected Cash Flow Details for Family

	2006	2007	2008
Cash Inflows			
Employment Inflows	263,925	273,162	180,167
Net Self-Employment Inflows	8,280	8,570	3,696
Investment Inflows	14,624	16,356	17,697
Pension Inflows	0	0	17,834
Miscellaneous Inflows	3,105	3,214	1,386
Received Capital	0	0	17,328
Total Cash Inflows	289,934	301,302	238,107
Cash Outflows			
Lifestyle Expenses	96,653	124,675	125,712
Taxes	95,048	100,058	61,018
Miscellaneous Expenses	12,780	13,222	13,680
Non-Qualified Contributions and Reinvestments	65,453	43,347	17,697
Qualified Contributions	20,000	20,000	20,000
Total Cash Outflows	289,934	301,302	238,107

Figure 6

Modeling Retirement Scenarios

Once you are comfortable that the data is correct and the assumptions are reasonable, and understand how the projections are being made, the fun part begins (at least for me this is fun!). This is where we can model different scenarios, duplicate the plan, make changes and view the results side-by-side for comparisons.

Let me give you a typical example. Let's say when you retire you want to buy a place in Florida to spend the winters. The questions arise: Can we afford to keep both houses? How much can we afford to spend on the second home? The planning software allows me to quickly duplicate the original plan with only one house; I then modify the second planning scenario "Buy Florida Condo Plan" and plug in some numbers that are different in this scenario. I input a $350,000 all cash purchase for the Florida condo; I reduce your investment portfolio by $350,000: I increase your expenses to simulate additional monthly costs for the Florida condo, real estate taxes, etc.

Now we can see both plans on the computer screen side-by-side for comparison. By making these changes with you while you are sitting and watching, you immediately see the effects on your cash flow and how it affects your total net worth. You become more involved in producing a plan that reflects your individual situation and the process helps you make better decisions because we were able to more accurately model your particular situation.

I have included the graphical output of both plans' net worth differences over time from the above scenario, (Figure 7). The Base Plan shows a current financial situation with just one home and with all current assumptions of assets, expenses, inflation and investment rate of return. I then duplicated the plan and only made the changes to reflect buying the condo in Florida. In the "Buy Florida Condo $350k Plan", you can see the difference this will have on your net worth over time. In this example by buying the Florida condo you will have approximately $358,000 less in net worth in 2016 and you will run out of money sooner than if you only had the expenses of one home. Maybe you should consider renting in Florida? That would require another scenario for us to model together.

Buy Florida Condo $350k

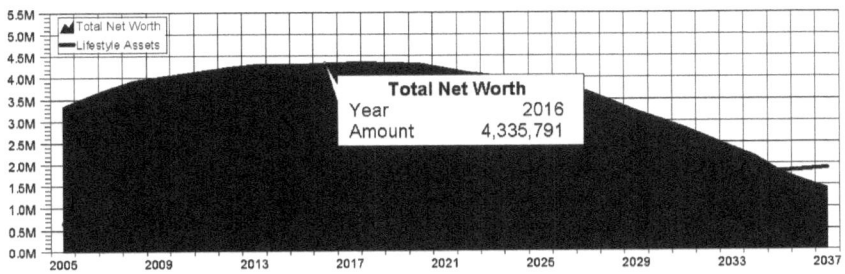

Base Plan

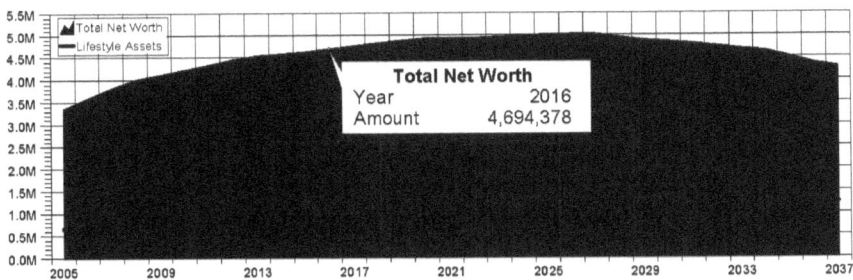

Figure 7

Please keep in mind that this requires very sophisticated modeling software which is difficult to use accurately, but the possibilities of providing a better overall retirement plan are greatly enhanced. Depending on what is trying to be answered (will my spouse be able to maintain her standard of living if I take the 50% survivor options on my pension and then I die in two years?), many scenarios can be compared. Usually we boil it down to two or three and most of the questions are answered.

Long Term Illness Scenario

One of the biggest concerns for the single RINK is, what happens to me if I get ill and need assistance for a few years? What if I need to go into an assisted living facility for a while or hire a geriatric care manager? Will I run out of money? Should I buy long-term care insurance or self-fund my medical payments? We have several ways of trying to show you how this expense will affect your total net worth.

Remember, your total net worth is your "retirement nest egg" that produces the income for you to live on along with social security and a pension, if any.

I took an existing client's plan and modified it to try and show you the affects of a very large health care expense, (Figure 8), for example, having a stroke but wanting to stay in your own home with around-the clock assistance. In these charts I used the plan of a single 70-year-old retired doctor who has only social security income. She had previously rolled her business pension plan into a large IRA. Most of her income stream comes from social security and withdrawals from her IRA, with a little money taken from her taxable investment accounts. Initially, I created a Base Plan, (middle of Figure 8), that illustrates her current situation: retired at age 70, in year 2006, her annual living expenses amount to about $90,000 a year; her total assets equal approximately $1,768,000 (all in liquid investments; she does not own a home); the assumed rate of inflation for the plan is 3% (except the health expense will be inflated at 3.5% a year) and for the return on her investments other than $300,000 sitting in a bank account the rest was in brokerage accounts that we assumed an aggressive 7% a year return.

Next I duplicated her plan exactly, creating a new plan entitled $100k Year Health Expenses 2010-2013, (bottom of Figure 8). In this plan I added a health care expense of $100,000 a year, (in today's dollars increasing with 3.5 inflation, because health care costs go up more than normal inflation) for 4 years, 2010-2013, to simulate a catastrophic health expense. Perhaps the plan illustrates a stroke where she might need to have around the clock assistance for 4 years but she wants to stay in her own home.

To give you an idea how inflation affects her expenses in retirement, the $100,000 a year health expense in today's dollars will be $114,752.30 in 2010. By the time she has paid her 4th year for her 2013 health expense it would cost her $127,227.93. The total expense for the four years would be $483,674. This is the amount that is required to be withdrawn *after taxes* to pay for this expense. You can see the income tax impact on the top chart, Projected Cash Flow Details of Figure 8. You should note that in 2013 the taxes are $150,468!

Next we pick a point in the future; in this case the year 2020, to compare what her net worth is then versus the base plan. In her case, she would have approximately $1,219,000 less in 2020 due to the very large health care expense. This expense also causes her to run out of money at around age 87, whereas in the base plan, she died at age 90 with about $1,600,000 still available in her estate.

Now you might say this doesn't make any sense. How could this short-term expense have such a negative impact on her net worth, especially when you used an aggressive average long-term rate of return on most of her investments of 7%?

This is where a sophisticated cash-flow based financial planning software package that has both federal and state income tax tables built in really helps. This retired doctor has the bulk of her assets in her IRA, which is quite typical of a medical doctor who tries to shelter as much of her income from taxes while she is working. When she retires she rolls this retirement plan into an IRA. What you might have forgotten about is the fact that, as she withdraws the money from her retirement account, she has to pay both federal and state income tax on the withdrawals at regular income tax rates.

By the time the doctor pays her 4th year of health expense in 2013, she must take all of her withdrawals from her IRAs, since she depleted her other savings. In 2013, she must withdraw

$416,000 from her IRAs, paying $150,000 in taxes, in order to have enough money to cover all of her then living expenses plus her health expense for the year. She ends up losing about 36 cents on every dollar to income taxes in that last year.

If you were in my office, I could show you the detailed numbers for each year and you would see exactly how the flow of your money comes in from social security and investments and goes out to expenses and taxes. The detailed cash flow projection would be too cumbersome to illustrate in this book. I have included a summary chart of the projected cash flow for the health emergency years.

Cash Flow Retirement Software Is Key

What I have illustrated is a very drastic scenario but not out of the question. I could have used a less expensive health care cost. For example, $30,000 a year for a part time aid for a few years, but the point I want to make is the kind of scenarios you can analyze with a good cash-flow driven software package, and the knowledge of how to use it. This might help you make decisions on whether to self-fund your long-term health care costs, get long-term care insurance, or possibly do some elder care planning with an elder law attorney. Once you receive some quotes on the cost of the long term care insurance you could create a scenario showing those annual expenses and compare that to other plans.

A financial planner has the resources to save the plans he has done with clients. When an important financial decision is to be made in the future or you just want to see where you currently stand, he can easily update your old plan with the new information.

Financial planning is not a one-time event; much like physical fitness: you can't do it once and expect to stay in shape. Your life situation is always changing as well as the economic climate, so you must regularly review and update your projections to ensure you are staying in good financial health. There is a lot of truth to the saying, "we plan and god laughs," so you need to remain flexible and ready to make smart money decisions as new life situations present themselves.

Projected Cash Flow Details

$100k Year Health Expenses 2010-2013 (2006)

	2009	2010	2011	2012	2013	2014
Cash Inflows						
Investment Inflows	19,075	60,240	66,196	71,387	1,499	0
Pension Inflows	55,577	59,294	63,253	67,467	416,645	130,227
Received Capital	23,518	105,910	106,129	105,963	1,981	0
Total Cash Inflows	98,169	225,444	235,577	244,817	420,125	130,227
Cash Outflows						
Lifestyle Expenses	83,504	200,761	207,358	214,172	269,660	96,804
Taxes	13,063	24,682	28,219	30,649	150,468	33,414
Non-Qualified Contributions and Reinvestments	1,603	0	0	0	0	0
Total Cash Outflows	98,169	225,443	235,576	244,821	420,128	130,218

Base Plan

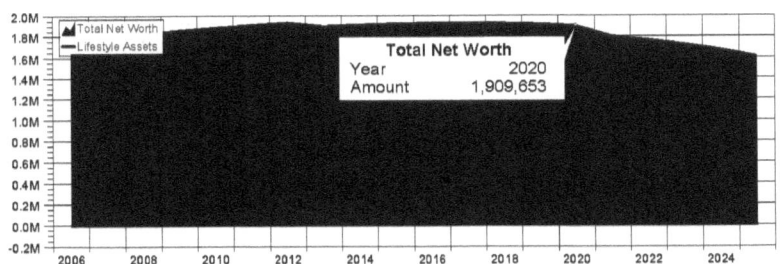

$100k Year Health Expenses 2010-2013

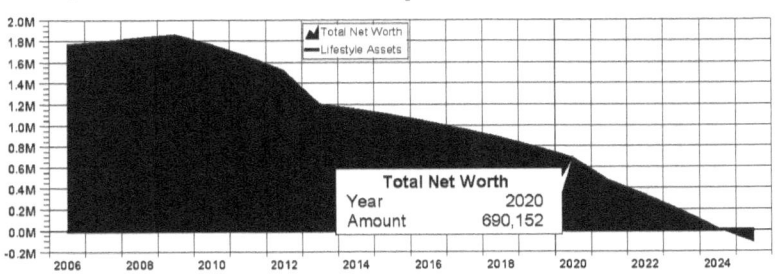

Figure 8

43

Assumed Rates of Return for Planning

Somewhere during this second planning meeting, I pursue a conversation on assumed rates of return produced from your investment portfolio. When I speak about your investment portfolio I am considering all of your investible assets, real estate, your bank accounts, CDs, bonds, stocks, and mutual funds from all sources, whether they are in a 401k plan or a regular taxable account. Deciding on what investment return to use is an extremely important topic that I will cover in detail in the chapter on investments, but, basically I need to spend time trying to understand the client's risk tolerance level.

At this stage we have a discussion on historical returns for balanced portfolios based on different risk levels. We are not trying to create an appropriate investment portfolio for the client (that comes later, as most clients want their investment portfolio professionally managed for them), but we are trying to determine the appropriate rate of return that should be used in the retirement projections. Simply stated, how much do we feel would be a fair average annual increase to expect each year from your investment portfolio if it were based on a particular chosen balanced strategy?

This can sometimes turn into a "what comes first, the chicken or the egg" question. Do we look at your current portfolio's overall mix and then decide, based on historical past returns, that in the future you should achieve an x% a year average return? Do we then plug that into the planning software to use in our projections? Or, do we input all of your income and expenses and then determine what rate of return you need, in order to sustain you throughout your long retirement?

Magical Returns Dial

One of the problems I have seen in the past, especially in the late nineties when the stock market was really doing well, was caused by some inexpensive financial planning software, which had what I called the "magical returns dial". The way it worked was: you put in how much you thought you needed each year to live on plus how much your total investible assets were, and then the output would show you if you had enough money or not. If it showed you did not have enough, no problem. The software tells you that you must have a more aggressive investment strategy to meet your needs so just turn the magical returns dial and increase your investment portfolio from moderate to very aggressive to increase from 6% a year to 11% a year returns and you can live happily ever after! Great, but guess what happened to the person who decided to retire early in 1999 based on this plan? He might be back working again, but this time at McDonalds.

SWAG It!

Here's how I like to arrive at the number to use and perhaps this will help you. First you must keep in mind that you are *guessing*. Yes, I said guessing, because if anyone can tell you what the stock and bond markets will return over the rest of your life then I think you must already be in heaven. While I don't just pick a number out of a hat, we need to look at several facts to arrive at "our guess" then monitor and adjust from there.

Of course, you won't hear your advisor tell you he is guessing since this seems amateurish and you are paying him good money to give you the real "facts". You know, that secret inside information that is only reserved for the $100 million clients! So instead of saying just *guessing,* the truly experienced advisors use a more professional process called *SWAG.* This stands for *Scientific Wild A** Guess* (my young nieces might read this book so I'll use **).

Of course I'm telling you about SWAG half kidding. The point is, for planning purposes you need a starting point when using expected rates of returns. This is part science and part art. An experienced advisor is applying much wisdom from reading volumes of studies on the subject when he comes up with the number.

Historical Returns

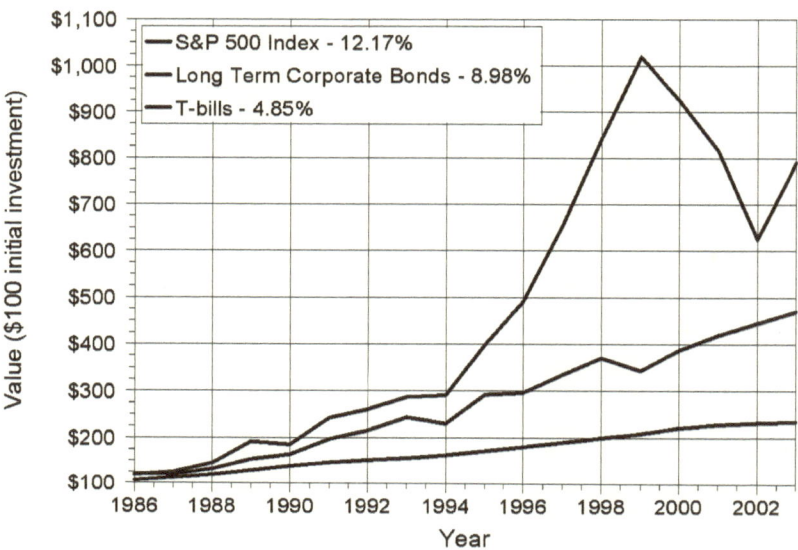

Year	S&P 500 Index (Rate)	Long Term Corporate Bonds (Rate)	T-bills (Rate)
1986	18.47%	19.85%	6.16%
1987	5.23%	-0.27%	5.47%
1988	16.81%	10.70%	6.35%
1989	31.49%	16.23%	8.37%
1990	-3.17%	6.78%	7.81%
1991	30.55%	19.89%	5.60%
1992	7.67%	9.39%	3.51%
1993	9.99%	13.19%	2.90%
1994	1.31%	-5.76%	3.90%
1995	37.43%	27.20%	5.60%
1996	23.07%	1.40%	5.21%
1997	33.36%	12.95%	5.26%
1998	28.58%	10.76%	4.86%
1999	21.04%	-7.45%	4.68%
2000	-9.11%	12.87%	5.89%
2001	-11.89%	8.23%	3.35%
2002	-23.37%	6.17%	1.63%
2003	26.38%	5.62%	1.05%

Figure 9

From the initial discussions with the client and having all of the facts of their financial life, including all of the investment statements, I can make an initial assessment of their investment style and tolerance for risk, based on my experience. This is very important because, if you are over 50 years old, I'm not about to try and change your *financial personality,* which has been developed in you since you had your first paper route or worked your first babysitting job. If you appear to have a somewhat *normal* investment personality, then I initially assume you can tolerate a *normal* amount of risk (I use the word "normal" very loosely here).

If a "normal" investment portfolio is a mix of 60% equities and 40% fixed income, we have to look at how this mix of investments has done in the past. Please keep in mind there are very big variations between what different people will put into the mix of investments that make up the 60/40 mix, but for this discussion, I'll assume it is a well-balanced, globally-diversified mix.

There are many sources of historical investment return information available from all of the large investment firms. Two sources I like to use are Ibbotson Associates in Chicago and Dimensional Fund Advisors in Santa Monica, California. Their data represents some of the most complete academic research that is currently available.

Use Past Investment Returns Intelligently

To give you an idea of what different investments have done historically, I have included (Figure 9), that shows the returns of stocks as represented by the S&P 500 Index, Bonds and T-bills. These charts of Historical Returns show the annual returns since 1986 and the graph shows how much you would have if you started out in 1986 with a $100 initial investment in each asset class.

We have all of this past historical data from different sources showing the annualized rates of return for a model Normal 60/40 mix for the last 5, 10 and 20 years. We think your investment personality will tolerate this normal mix, but I still don't just use the past returns. Why? First, you need to understand if the model strategy returns are based on pure asset class market returns without expenses. Most are. Therefore, you have to subtract some reasonable amount of expenses to actually invest in funds to make up this strategy, let's say we take off 1.25% a year from the returns.

Next you have to think about the investment environment that existed during the period that produced these returns. This is important and helpful in trying to estimate what the future investment environment will bring.

Are you looking at the returns of the Normal portfolio over a 10-year period that started out in a high interest-rate environment and ended in a low interest rate environment?

In that case, 40% of your portfolio invested in fixed income (bonds) would have had large returns due to the higher starting yields and the bond appreciation that occurs when interest rates drop. You have to ask your-self will the fixed income portion of the Normal portfolio perform the same over the next 10 years? Does the current climate appear to be the same (high interest rates)? Or is it different and bonds will react differently? If you are currently in a low interest rate environment and expect rising interest rates you should dampen your expectations from the fixed income portion of the Normal portfolio and lower your future expected returns.

The same would hold true with the 60% of equities in the Normal portfolio. If the last 10 years was, on average, a good equity return market and the returns produced from the equity portion of the balanced portfolio were 13% a year, is that likely to continue? You must think about the current investment environment and make some intelligent adjustments to your expected equity returns. If you believe the market is very undervalued and has been in a bear market for the last 3 years, perhaps your long-term expectation should be shifted higher. If you are just coming off of a 5-year bull market with high overall valuations, then perhaps you need to dampen your expectations going forward. As you can see, the process of trying to predict future returns requires knowledge of economic market fundamentals and a good dosage of SWAG.

Start With Your Initial Projection

I discuss more about this in the chapter on portfolio construction but the above comments are some of the issues you must think about prior to just plugging in a return number for your retirement planning projections. I try to evaluate your investment personality, know what the past returns have been for different model portfolios and make adjustments based on the current economic environment and asset class valuations to come up with an educated guess of a number, say 6% (I'm not recommending using 6%; since this is just for discussion). The assumption here is that you, the client, will adjust your investments to match the diversified portfolio needed to produce this number.

This initial number of 6% is what I plug into the plan and we analyze and discuss the results. Many times the client says let's use a lower number to be conservative and see if I'm still able to have enough money during the rest of my life. This is accomplished easily by duplicating the plan and leaving everything else the same except changing the return rates on the investments.

Don't Skew The Data Too Much

I have noticed that some people think that they are doing better planning if they skew all of the numbers one way or another. Don't do it! Sometimes they do this to make the projections very conservative and sometimes it's to convince their spouse to either stop working or continue working. If you fudge your expenses higher or estimate too low on your business income, then we have incorrect plan input data on which we are making projections and decisions.

Please, especially if you are working with a planner, try to give the planner the most accurate information that you have. The time to make adjustments to see if the plan will work out with lower returns or higher expenses is now, at this stage of the planning, *once you have established an accurate base plan.*

What Just 2% a Year Can Do

In the top graph (Figure 10), I have created a retirement plan for Dick and Jane with a 6% average rate of return. Based on their expenses, income and asset levels they will not run out of money during their lifetime. The net worth graph shows them with a projected net worth of just under $4,000,000 in the year 2026. In the next graph, (bottom of Figure 10), I duplicated the plan and left everything the same except I lowered the return rate to 4% on all of their investments. As you can see in the 4% plan, they run out of money during Jane's lifetime. In the year 2026, their total net worth is only about $2,300,000.

Keep in mind the plan is taking into consideration all the other usual elements such as inflation, taxes, etc. Most people don't realize until they see it in a graph how much of a difference just 2% a year in investment returns makes in compounding your money over your lifetime. This is why proper management of your investments is so critical to your successful retirement.

Plan With 6% Returns

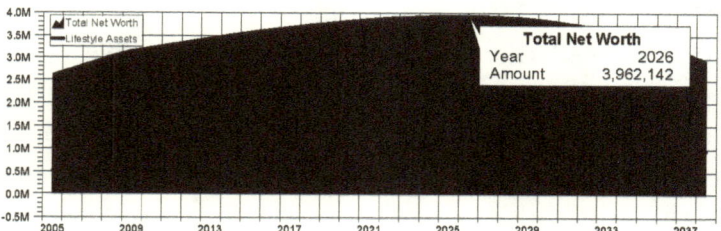

Plan With 4% Returns

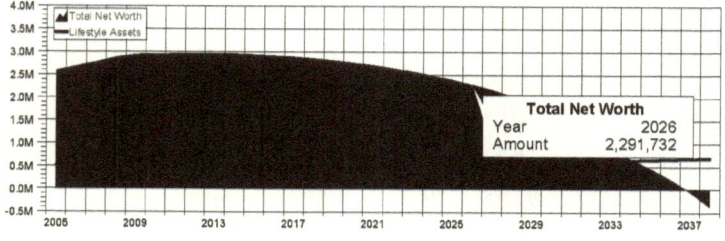

Figure 10

Review Real Results vs. Projections

The investment return decision is a very important decision and I usually show several different rates of returns to see if the plan still works. I will run what is called a Monte Carlo Simulation, which takes your current plan data and varies the return rates to simulate various non-linear market conditions as another means to "stress test" the validity or worthiness of the assumptions in your retirement plan. Various methods of testing the plan help towards building confidence that the retirement plan has a high degree of success.

The selection of the initial annualized rate of return in your projections is the first look at your future expectations. What I do with our clients is to go back every few years and compare the actual returns achieved on the investments to what was used in the original projections. This is critical and a key step in achieving good wealth management. There should be accountability in making sure the actual investment returns achieved, meet or exceed the projections used in your retirement planning.

Think about it: what is really important to you in any given year; beating the S&P 500 if the index lost 20% and you *only* lost 15%, or staying on track to meet your goals? Reviewing the investment results in coordination with your retirement projections is an ongoing discipline that, unfortunately, most retirees or, for that matter, most investment advisors, do not do. The reason this is so important is that it gives you a chance to make adjustments before your financial situation gets too far off course (or, if your investments are performing much better than the expectations, perhaps you will need to go on more vacations!).

There are many issues that come up during the second meeting that will need to be tracked to be sure they get resolved. Many of these will be covered in other chapters, but, as far as the planning process is concerned, the second meeting ends and I review the scenarios, generate appropriate reports and write a cover letter summarizing the main points of the retirement plan, its strengths and weaknesses.

Third Retirement Planning Meeting

This meeting is more of a review and summary of all the issues that were covered in the last meeting and many times the third meeting will involve a discussion on the investment policy. Since the previous meeting I have analyzed the different scenarios and ensured that all of the projections appeared to be correct. The most important reports are printed which show in detail the major areas of concern that came up in our discussions. In many cases I produce several alternative scenarios so that you can review the printed copies when you return home and digest them at your leisure.

In the plan cover letter I discuss the major points of the retirement analysis and compile a list of action items. These are items that should be implemented in order for the plan (your retirement) to be successful as the projections show. In many cases recommendations for additional services will be made such as the need for some complicated estate planning, charitable planning or long-term care insurance.

It is at this stage of the planning process that commissioned paid sales advisors will make recommendations for products or services in which they may make a very large commission. If you follow my advice in the chapter on selecting a trusted financial advisor and he is truly a Fee-Only planner, you will be confident that he is giving you objective advice. Since he does not sell products or receive any referral fees for recommendations, and since you could use any professional you choose to implement the needed services, you should have a higher degree of confidence that the recommendation was objective and only in your best interest.

Pending Action Items Checklist

In addition to the plan cover letter, I usually email a summary of the important points and a Pending Action Item Checklist showing who is responsible for each follow-up item, either you or the planner. Also on our website in each client's private area we post certain specific planning reports including the Pending Action Item list, budget sheet, net worth statement, etc.

The benefit of this is that during the year when the client signs on to view her portfolio quarterly reports or year-end tax reports, she is reminded of what needs to be done next in her planning process. The next time we have a review meeting, the reports on the website are updated. This is especially helpful for our out-of-state clients with whom we may do the planning almost entirely on the phone along with a Web meeting. Just as an added protection, since privacy and identity theft is a great concern, any client reports we post to our website are behind a password-protected area and we eliminate all client names, addresses and account numbers from the reports.

If you do the planning for yourself, you should keep a list of action items that you must be sure to follow up on. It is very easy to do all of the planning and determine all of the things you need to change or implement, and then put the list in your desk drawer and forget about it. You need to have the discipline to stick with the process, because you won't be getting calls from your planner reminding you.

Good Portfolio Performance Is Important

The successful retirement plan relies in a large part on your portfolio or nest egg providing good investment returns throughout your lifetime. You might not think about this too much while you are working and still saving, but once you retire your nest egg has to work for you. The ability of the investments to be properly managed so as to provide steady-risk adjusted returns will mean the difference of your money lasting your lifetime or not. This is especially important if you don't have a pension check coming in steadily each month but you must manage your own large sums of money which originated with the rollover of your 401(k) or 403(b) plan into your IRA.

It is usually recommended that a client consider having his portfolio professionally managed. In most cases, this will provide much better long-term returns and eliminate a lot of costly mistakes. The larger the amount of money you have, the more important it is to have it managed successfully. You can have your managed investment portfolios set up to provide automatic monthly deposits into your checking account based on the cash flow/budget needs you determined in the retirement planning process. Many people who don't have a steady pension check other than Social Security like this idea of a monthly deposit so they can budget their monthly expenses. I will discuss the investment management process in another chapter.

Most clients leave the last retirement planning meeting with a binder full of reports and with a lot more confidence that they have enough information to make good intelligent retirement decisions. They also take comfort in the knowledge that they have a sound strategy to take them forward into a life of retirement without having to worry about the unknown. While the reports in the binder are outdated very quickly, we have started a solid foundation of the ongoing process of monitoring and adjusting your wealth throughout your lifetime.

Chapter Summary

In this chapter I described some of the issues that I would cover with my own clients during the retirement planning process in order for you to understand the issues you must consider when you work with a financial planner or you do your own planning.

If you decide to work with a planner, you should be prepared to bring all of your financial documentation and be willing to share the information with the planner. In addition, the planner needs to get to understand you, your goals and financial anxieties in order to make good recommendations for you.

I illustrated that by using a good cash-flow driven financial planning software program, you can model many different scenarios accurately, taking into consideration the effects of taxes. In planning, you must assume an average rate of return on your investments as a starting point. In choosing this return rate, I suggested this be a combination of understanding your own investment personality, past historical market returns data, the current economic environment, future expectations from current valuations, and putting that all together with SWAG to arrive at your initial return rate.

You must continue to monitor your plan, comparing your assumptions with your actual results each year. This is important since investment performance is a key ingredient to the RINK's successful retirement. If your investment returns are not keeping up with the plan's initial projections, you must make adjustments to either your portfolio or spending in order to keep your retirement on a sound financial track.

5) Know Your Investing Personality

Don't fight forces; use them.
-R. Buckminster Fuller

What Kind Of Investor Are You?

In the previous chapter I discussed the need for proper retirement planning and how important it is to help you make smart retirement decisions. One of the most important parts of the plan is the assumption used for the investment returns. Simply, how much will your money grow to allow you to make your needed withdrawals to maintain your lifestyle? How your money was invested during your working career was important, but most successful people live off earned income prior to retirement and not from their savings and investments. How your money is invested and managed is critical early in retirement especially for the RINK who will need to cover additional expenses later in retirement.

It is interesting to me when I meet prospective clients for the first interview how two different people, each with the same basic lifetime wages and annual savings, can end up with such different-sized nest eggs at retirement. As I mentioned before, when you don't have children to raise and put through college, you have the potential to accumulate significant wealth.

I am not talking about the differences between spenders and savers, but the difference between smart investors and not-so-educated investors. Over a 30-40 year period of working and saving, someone with just modest investment skills can have 3 to 4 times the amount of total assets than someone who invested poorly. Let me be clear. I am talking about people who had similar incomes and expenses during their lifetimes and sacrificed and saved about the same each year. What they did with the money that was accumulated each year made the difference.

Why should one person end up with a $500,000 retirement nest egg and the other with $2,000,000 at the start of retirement? All right, you say, that's in the past; we did our net worth statement and this is what we have. This is very true, but understanding smarter ways of investing and how money compounds is more critical at the *beginning* of your retirement. Remember that you won't have any children to take care of you in your old age if you run out of money. I would like to group the four categories of investors that I have run across at the start of retirement. You should think about which category you (would possibly) fit into.

Successful Investor

I use this term to define someone I see that has accumulated significant wealth, which is mostly (from the result of) good saving and investing characteristics. The way to tell a successful investor is by simply discussing investments and reviewing their current portfolio. The key traits are usually these:

Humility: knowing that no one can consistently outsmart the market.

Cost Conscious: didn't waste a lot of money buying expensive low return insurance products, variable annuities, loaded mutual funds or other investment products that paid the sales person high commissions.

Disciplined: understood the amount of risk that could be tolerated and invested in both up and down markets in a well-diversified portfolio of low cost mutual funds or bonds.

Devoted time*:* regularly to reading and understanding investing fundamentals.

Even temperament*:* is not swayed by fear or greed and avoided making irrational (expensive), impulsive investment decisions.

Average IQ: while some people believe the brightest people make the best investors, I have found the opposite to be true in non-professional investors. It seems the people who are the brightest professionals believe that since they are so good in their own professional field, they should be able to outsmart the market. In their quest to do better than everyone else, they constantly make bad decisions. I have seen this tendency in very bright and successful attorneys and physicians, for example.

The successful investor usually ends up with a larger net worth upon retirement than the less-successful investor who had a comparable income. Time and the compounding of money are in the successful investor's favor.

Average Investor

To me the average investor is someone who has always believed in investing and due to the natural upward movement of global stock and bond markets has done ok. Some traits are:

No overall investment strategy: a mixed bag of different investments acquired at different times for unknown reasons.

Usually invested the maximum to his retirement plan each year but always tried moving to the best performing plan selections from the last quarter's performance report.

Allowed the emotions of fear and greed to affect his judgment and make poor market timing decisions over the years. Invests more money at market peaks and moves to cash during prolonged bear markets.

Spend more time tracking and monitoring the investments than trying to understand investing fundamentals.

The success of the average investor has been helped greatly by the long bull market from 1982 to 1999 and therefore he has several times the net worth of the Ultra Conservative CD only saver. The environment since 1999 hasn't been as kind to the average investor. Disciplined savings has been the main wealth accumulation driver here.

Ultra-Conservative Investor

This is the investor for whom I feel sorry. In many cases the ultra-conservative investor is a child of parents who went through the Depression. He is so fearful of taking risk that by playing it "safe" he actually puts a successful retirement on weak financial footing. Some traits are:

Didn't trust anyone, wanted to be sure his hard earned money was FDIC-insured in a bank.

Kept wishing for the high interest rates and free TVs given with each new CD opened. (I remember my grandmother opened a CD for each of her nine grandchildren because she received a free ticket to the 1965 World's Fair for each CD. She was thrilled and so were we!)

Wouldn't invest in any bonds except EE savings bonds.

The end result is that, while the ultra- conservative investor may have a sizable nest egg, it is anywhere from 1/3 to 1/5 of what it could have been with just a little tolerance for risk.

Foolish Investor

Up until the tech/Internet crazy market of 1999 and early 2000 this was a rare breed. But the siren song of making 100% return on your money in less than a year created an entire crop of foolish investors. In a short period of time they lost a very large percentage of their retirement nest egg to greed driven behavior.

Common traits:

Spent a significant amount of time on the Internet or ***watching for hot tips*** on CNBC or any number of the market newsletters to which he subscribes.

Allowed greed to take over his personality and made huge bets in overly priced stocks, usually as they peaked. Then stubbornly held them forever, although there were very low odds of recouping the initial investment.

Bragged a lot to his friends when one of his investments did well yet didn't bring up the stock market at all when he was doing badly (which was usually more often than he even realized).

Usually had a broker who encouraged the use of margin so that the losses were magnified many times over. The broker assured him everyone else was getting killed, not just he (maybe all of that broker's other clients were anyway).

The profile of the foolish investor cannot be stereotyped. I've seen homemakers, businessmen, and professionals. It doesn't seem to matter. The thing they all have in common is that they all sadly reduced their nest egg by 50% or more. Now they and (usually their unknowing spouse) will not be able to retire when they wanted to and their entire retirement lifestyle will be significantly reduced and will usually be much lower than their current lifestyle.

As an aside, the truly bigger tragedy is that in many cases there are still enough assets to create a good diversified retirement portfolio but the foolish investor wants to hold on to his current investments until they "go back to what I paid for them and then we can sell them", maybe in the next life.

Your Portfolio In Retirement

The reason I discussed the above investment personalities is because understanding your own history and experience is very important in making good investment decisions at the beginning of the retirement stage of your life's journey. You should determine what type of investor you have been and decide if you should go forward on your own or seek professional money management.

In my experience the average person does more harm to his long-term retirement investment returns because of over confidence in his own ability and by making bad, emotional short-term decisions. In some instances he changes brokers or investment advisors every year in a self-defeating effort to achieve the best possible yearly performance. A good professional advisor will keep your strategy focused on steady long-term results and tune out short-term market "noise". Short-term market "noise" is current news reports and media coverage that seems important at the time but has very little long-term impact on the growth of the economy and your investments. In the next chapter I will discuss investments in more detail.

Benefits of Consolidation

In order to create a successful investment portfolio, you need to take all of your liquid assets into consideration when constructing your investment strategy. This is important because it allows you to better visualize your overall asset allocation and control your risk. The best way to accomplish this is by consolidating all of your investments in a discount brokerage firm that has a supermarket platform of mutual funds available for you. I suggest TD Ameritrade, Charles Schwab, Vanguard or Fidelity.

It is difficult to manage money properly as it is. Please make it easier by consolidating. This means putting your stock certificates in your brokerage account. Transfer all of your stocks, mutual funds and individual bonds to the one firm. You may still have several actual brokerage accounts such as a joint, individual, Trust, IRA, Roth IRA etc. but at least they are located at one firm. Sometimes the brokerage firm you are leaving will charge you a small fee. In most cases mutual fund companies will not charge you a fee to transfer the assets over and the receiving brokerage firm will assist you with the paper work. Most mutual funds can be transferred between firms with no problem; I know TD Ameritrade accepts about 10,000 different mutual funds.

Besides making proper money management easier. There are many other benefits. Since they are all on one statement, your heirs will have fewer headaches trying to determine where all of your assets are. They will thank you and love you for making it easier for them. This is especially important if you don't have a surviving spouse or partner who knows where all of your assets are located.

People with children usually have one of the children as executor of the estate and keep them informed of where all investments are located. Without children or a spouse you make it much easier for whomever you choose to handle your affairs if you have all of your liquid investments consolidated.

Consolidation Simplifies Tax Preparation

Since your consolidated brokerage account automatically has a money market fund tied to it all of your dividends flow into your money market and collect interest immediately. No more lost checks and trips to the bank! You get consolidated monthly statements of all the activities in the account so you can easily follow what has transpired (dividend, interest payments, stock splits etc.). Your tax preparer will love it since you will have a consolidated 1099 with all the taxable activity in one place (he may even charge you less).

Most discount brokers don't charge any fee to keep your account open. They can arrange for automatic monthly deposits into your bank account. It simply makes your financial life that much more organized. You can also have web access to all of your accounts with the discount broker if you want.

Use Software To Manage Investments

In most cases you cannot consolidate 100% of your assets since you may have some bank CDs, annuities, or life insurance policies that must remain with the provider. You still need to track all of these investments in order to create a properly diversified portfolio. If you are comfortable working with the computer, then you should use a program such as Quicken to enable you to track all of your investments, no matter where they are located. The better organized you are, the clearer your investment decisions will be.

At my firm we use a sophisticated portfolio management program that receives a download every morning from our custodian. All activity is loaded into our clients' accounts. It updates prices, trades, dividends and tax-cost basis. If a client has investments located elsewhere, we manually bring that data into our program and integrate it so we can see all of the client's investments as one portfolio. The idea is to be able on one screen to view all of your investments together so that we can make better asset allocation and investment decisions. I can't stress enough how important this is for your money management.

It wouldn't make economic sense for you to buy an expensive portfolio management program like we have. If you can learn to use something like Quicken or an Excel spreadsheet you could come close to accomplishing the same thing. (Of course you will spend a lot of time manually entering information, not much fun).

Chapter Summary

Retiring without children means you have to rely more on your money to provide for your needs in retirement. Proper management of your investments is critical if the money is to last during your long retirement. Knowing your investment personality and how you behaved in past bull and bear markets is a good indicator of your future investment behavior.

Now is not the time to be overconfident in your investment abilities since a successful outcome is too critical. If you feel you can continue to manage your investments and have done a good job in the past, then by all means continue. If not, consider working with a good professional advisor. I will explain how to evaluate financial advisors in another chapter. For now, let's move on to discuss investments.

6) Investing Basics

He who wishes to be rich in a day will be hanged in a year.
-Leonardo da Vinci

In the prior chapter we discussed different investment personalities and how, with all other things being equal, a successful investor may have accumulated much more in assets than a very conservative investor or a foolish investor. The portfolio (the aggregation of all of your investments) will be the RINK's safety net in retirement. Before we can discuss creating an intelligently-diversified, globally-strategic portfolio, let's cover some investment basics. If you already are an experienced investor you might want to skip this chapter. Let's put aside your privately-owned real estate, businesses or private partnerships for now and in its simplest form let me discuss investing in two basic categories: equities and fixed income.

Equities Are For Growth

With equities you own shares of a company, usually in the form of a marketable security, or a common stock. Your part-ownership in the company may give you certain rewards such as additional shares or cash dividends the company may pay out. You are a fractional owner in the company that is your equity. You typically won't own enough of a public company to have much say in how it runs other than voting your proxy each year.

Your share of the company or your individual stock most likely will trade on one of the major stock exchanges: NYSE, AMEX or NASDAQ. The exchange provides a service matching up buyers with sellers. Your shares will be an entry on your monthly brokerage statement showing how many shares of the company you own. The main reason you want to own equities or stocks (I will discuss how the best way to own them is via mutual funds) is so that you can participate in both the growth of the company and the future dividends that may be paid to shareholders. If the company increases its earnings each year other investors will bid up the price of the company's shares and, therefore, your shares will be worth more.

The value of your shares in a public company is priced everyday in the public market and you have very little control over the price movement. While as a part owner of the company you participate in the success of the company you also have the risk that your investment could decline if the company doesn't do well and the value of your shares decrease. An equity owner is willing to take the risk of a fluctuating market value in order to participate in the potential growth of the company.

Fixed Income For Safety

When we talk about fixed income investments we usually mean a vehicle that you own that lends money out. Instead of being an owner of the company, as you are with the equities, with fixed-income investments you are basically lending your money, which makes you a creditor. Some of the most common types of lending vehicles are bonds, Certificates of Deposits (CDs) and fixed annuities. With fixed income FI you are loaning your money to a company, bank or government agency for a fixed payout rate in the form of an interest payment to you and upon the maturity of the investment you would get the face value of the bond returned back to you.

The initial interest or coupon rate of the bond is set by the borrower and the governing instrument. It is based usually by current market conditions and usually doesn't change after your purchase. You are lending your money for their specific needs. Traditional borrowers will invest the funds at rates of return higher than what they pay you, making a profit on the spread. Other borrowers such as government or municipal agencies will use your loans for specific uses; they are in the money spending business not a moneymaking business.

Bonds are usually purchased from bond dealers who set current prices based on the safety rating of the bond, the length of time until maturity of the bond and current interest rates. The markup or commission on individual bonds is pretty high for individual investors, and I believe, for the average investor, bonds are best purchased via low-cost bond mutual funds.

As a lender your risk is far less than as an equity owner, especially if you stick with very safe fixed income investments, such as AAA-rated or government-insured bonds. There are also fixed-income investments that can have a high risk of default (remember MCI bonds), yet the biggest risk you face as a fixed income investor is usually the decline from market pricing of your bonds due to changes in interest rates.

Most people incorrectly believe the role of fixed income investments in their portfolio is to provide a stream of income, which they do, but the primary role of having fixed-income investments in a portfolio is to dampen the overall volatility of your portfolio (the volatility comes from your equity positions).

Bonds

I want to explain a little more about bonds since they are the primary component of most people's fixed-income exposure and, while many people seem to understand individual stocks, they have a harder time understanding individual bonds or bond funds.

You now know that as a bondholder you are a lender; you lend your money to a debtor such as the U.S. Government, a municipal school system or a corporation. In return for lending your money for a fixed period of years, you get the promise of fixed interest payments each year. The payment to you, usually every six months, are called *coupons.* The amount you loaned to the company, for example, $10,000, is your *principal* that you expect to get back when the bond comes due upon maturity. In a very simple example a bond purchased at par for $10,000 due in 10 years paying 7% a year semiannually will pay you $350 of interest every six months. A total of $700 for the year.

While this example may seem simple to you, in reality bonds can get much more complicated. Since many bonds are not purchased at par or the nice even $10,000. Most bonds are purchased on the secondary market and their prices are either above or below par. A bond which costs more than the issue price ($10,000) is said to be selling at a *premium* while one selling below issue price (or par) is said to be selling at a *discount.*

Some of the things that affect the bond's price are current interest rates, changes in credit rating of the issuer, and time left until maturity of the bond. Once a bond is issued, its value fluctuates and this fluctuation determines the current yield that you will receive. The 7% coupon bond selling at a discount will yield more than 7% while one selling at a premium will yield less than 7%.

To obtain the current yield, you divide the bond's annual interest by its current trading price. If the trading price of your $10,000 par bond with a simple yield of 7 percent declined to $8,500, for instance, the current yield would rise to 8.2% ($700 divided by $8,500). The coupon payout stays constant in dollars while the value of the bond changes. What this means is that the investor who paid $10,000 received a 7% yield while the investor who purchased the bond for the discounted price of $8,500 will have a current yield of 8.2%.

Interest Rates Affect Bond Values

Changes in interest rates have the most effect on the value of your bonds. When overall market interest rates go lower because of changes in the economic environment, your bond positions actually increase in value; on the other hand when interest rates begin to rise, your bond positions will decline in value. The longer the term to maturity your bond has, the more the value of the bond will drop with rising interest rates. This inverse relationship between interest rates and the value of bond positions seems to be the hardest concept most people have in understanding bonds.

Trying to determine the best bonds to buy at any given time can get very complicated because there are many other issues that come into play that are beyond the scope of this book. There are many variations of bonds and fixed income investments, inflation-indexed bonds, mortgage-backed bonds, junk bonds, zero coupon bonds, municipal bonds and many more.

If you are selecting individual bond positions you really need to know what you are doing. In most cases, you are much better off using a good, low-cost bond mutual fund for your bond portfolio but, even then, you need to understand some bond basics in order to understand what benefits the bond mutual fund will provide and what your risks are.

Use Low Cost Mutual Funds

As I have been hinting at so far, I believe no-load or institutional low-cost mutual funds are most people's best way to invest in both the equity and fixed-income market. Institutional class mutual funds are mutual funds that have very low expenses and are usually only available with very large purchases say $100,000 or more. A mutual fund is a company that pools money from many investors and uses that pooled money to purchase a portfolio of stocks, bonds or other investments according to the terms outlined in its *prospectus*.

The prospectus defines the objectives and expenses of the mutual fund and is filed with the Securities and Exchange Commission

(SEC). The SEC has rules governing mutual funds and the mutual fund companies are required to abide by these rules. Mutual funds invest according to specific objectives such as income or growth and income, if you invest in a short-term domestic bond fund, you wouldn't expect to find international stocks in that mutual fund unless that was allowed in the prospectus.

The benefits of mutual funds include simplicity and diversification. With one purchase you can get a mutual fund that invests in hundreds of stocks or bonds. You also get professional management of the investments within the mutual fund if it is an actively managed mutual fund (I will discuss active vs. passive management later).

Selecting Mutual Funds

The selection of mutual funds in building your retirement portfolio is not an easy task since there are now more mutual funds than individual stocks on the New York Stock Exchange. Services such as Morningstar, Lipper and Value Line rate mutual funds and you need to understand the criteria these services use in the evaluation of the mutual funds.

While the past performance of the mutual fund is important, it is just one criteria you should evaluate. More importantly, you need to understand the investments inside the mutual fund to understand its past performance. Also, to know if it agrees with your macro view of how those investments might do going forward.

For example, if you purchased a technology fund in January of 2001 (just before technology stocks tanked) based just on its past five years performance record, you most likely made a very expensive mistake. Similarly, if you purchased a bond fund because its last five years' total returns were great and didn't understand that those returns were great because the mutual fund held very long term bonds in a falling interest rate environment, you could be making a big mistake. Why? Because, if interest rates now started to rise, you could suffer fairly significant losses in a bond fund that you thought had a good record and was safe.

Mutual Fund Sales Fees

There are a few general pointers you should consider when purchasing mutual funds. You want to avoid paying sales charges when purchasing a mutual fund; these sales charges are sometimes called *Loads*. You also want to use mutual funds that have low internal expenses when possible. By avoiding loads and high internal expenses you will have a head start in getting good investment returns.

Sales charges come in different variations. They are commissions paid to a stockbroker or financial planner who works on commissions (I will discuss different compensation methods of financial advisors later). In most cases, these should be avoided unless the advisor you are working with is providing you with some other ongoing advice.

Load funds come in many variations. The variations all have to do with how the commission is paid, not how the fund performs. Some of the more common variations are:

A front-end load, called class A; you will see the letter following the fund in the newspaper. Class A funds are sold with an upfront commission say 5% and usually have a .25% a year commission paid to the advisor. If you have to buy a load fund over the long haul the Class A fund may be your best bet.

A back end load Class B; doesn't have a front end sales charge but will charge you a fee if you sell the fund before a set number of years, which is explained in the prospectus (usually five years). It also has very high 12b-1 annual trail fees each year. A 12b-1 fee is a marketing fee commonly added to load funds. These funds usually end up costing you more than Class A funds over the long run.

A level load Class C; doesn't have a front-end charge and may only have a back end charge within the first year, but has a higher ongoing charge each year. This could end up costing you the most money.

The only reason you should be purchasing a mutual fund with a sales load is if you have an established relationship with a financial advisor who is commissioned based and you understand what other services the advisor will be providing for you. Even then, you need to understand which class of load is best for you.

Mutual Fund Ongoing Expenses

You should also be concerned with the ongoing management expenses of the mutual fund you are looking to buy since, with all other things being equal, high expenses will reduce your investment returns. Mutual fund expenses are the fees that the mutual fund company charges as a percentage of the money they manage. These expense fees are how mutual fund companies cover expenses and make profits.

These costs are referred to as expense ratios and can range from about .25% to 2% or more per year and in effect, they reduce the total investment return your mutual fund has earned.

For example, let's compare two different funds. Before fees, both have a return on investments of 10%. If fund A charges .5% per year in expenses, you end up with a return of 9.5%. If fund B has an expense ratio of 1.5%, you end up with a return of only 8.5% for the year. If you invested $100,000 at the beginning of the year and both funds made a gain of 10% on investments before expenses, at the end of the year, you would have $109,500 in fund A and you would have just $108,500 in fund B.

Over a lifetime of investing, with all other things being equal, you will end up with more wealth if you stick with mutual funds with lower expenses. There are institutional class mutual funds that have very low expense ratios that aren't available to the retail buyer, but a Fee-Only advisor can usually purchase these funds for his clients, thus saving the clients money over the long run. In addition, many times a Fee-Only investment advisor can purchase funds that normally sell with a sales load, without the sales load for his clients.

ETFs

The last type of investment vehicle I would like to cover in this chapter is Exchange Traded Funds (ETFs). ETFs trade as stocks but are in effect a fund of stocks. ETFs were introduced back in the early 1990s and have only recently become more popular. I started using them for my clients several years ago and I think when you understand how they work you will see why these make great investment vehicles.

There are currently well over 100 different ETFs available, with new ones being introduced almost everyday; most ETFs track the popular stock market indexes. Some of the most popular are the Spiders (SPY), which tracks the S & P 500 index, the Quebes (QQQQ), which tracks the NASDAQ 100 index, and the I Share Russell 2000 (IWM) which tracks the small cap Russell 2000 index.

ETFs allow you in one transaction to purchase a basket of many stocks (depending on the index it tracks) so you get great diversification in one investment. In addition ETFs have very low expense ratios; most charge .25% a year or less, which could be 1/5 the cost of a typical actively- managed mutual fund. Because of the way ETFs are constructed, they are very tax-efficient: while the typical mutual fund at times will distribute hefty taxable capital gains distributions at year end, ETFs generally distribute little if any capital gains. For this reason, they make good sense as a core holding in a taxable account and I'll discuss their use in portfolio construction a little later.

Chapter Summary

Hopefully this chapter gave you a little refresher course on some investment building blocks. Your investment portfolio should be composed of equity and fixed-income investments. The equities provide you with long-term growth and the fixed income investments provide safety and lessen portfolio volatility.

When you own equities you are an owner in the company and when you own fixed income (bonds) you are a lender and receive interest payments. Bonds are not as simple as they appear to understand since their prices change due to interest rates and other factors. I believe you would be best served by buying stocks and bonds through low-cost mutual funds.

When purchasing mutual funds understand the sales charges and internal expenses of the funds before purchasing. You should avoid funds with high expenses and sales charges unless your advisor is providing other value to you.

ETFs are a good way to participate in the equity markets since they have low costs and are very tax-efficient. Next, we'll discuss putting together an investment portfolio to take you through retirement.

7) Portfolio Construction

For all long-term investors, there is only one objective-
maximum total return after taxes.
-Sir John Templeton

Creating and maintaining an intelligently diversified portfolio of investments is critical to your ability to remain independent with dignity during retirement. The initial selection and ongoing management of your portfolio is very important to fulfill your monthly retirement/withdrawal needs. It will also allow you to maintain the large financial cushion that RINKs need to buffer against future emergency medical needs. Lastly, a well-managed portfolio is important if you have any desire to leave an inheritance to relatives or certain charities.

Prior to the construction of your investment portfolio you need to do a complete financial analysis to determine what you need your portfolio to accomplish for you. **"Hey, Ray I want my portfolio to make as much money as possible but never go down,"** is not a realistic strategy for creating a portfolio, although this is how some people think.

Once your goals, needs and safe portfolio withdrawal rates are determined, you have to understand your ability to accept risk.

You need to think long and hard about the question of risk, since this drives your investment strategy and therefore your long-term investment returns.

What Is The Portfolio For?

Many people with children, although retired, usually spend a good portion of their yearly income on their children and grandchildren in the form of gifts or taking them on vacations. I have clients who are in their 80s and are still subsidizing their adult children's lifestyles while sacrificing their own spending.

The RINK is not burdened with these issues but has other items to consider. Do you have financial commitments supporting an aging parent or sibling? Do you, your spouse or partner have known health issues that will create the need for large cash outlays? While all of these issues should be flushed out when first doing your financial and retirement planning, they need to be taken into consideration when you are trying to determine how much risk you need, or are willing to take, in the design of your investment strategy.

Portfolio Risk

What does *risk* mean and how is it defined? Let me present you with some definitions of risk that people have.

Risk of loss: you don't want to experience a loss. You define risk as losing money, so you may feel that if you don't lose money on an investment, even if the return is substandard, there is no risk involved in the equation.

Risk of variability: how much will an investment's actual return differ from the expected return. This applies to portfolio design.

Risk as the failure to achieve specific financial goals: is your greatest risk and the one from which we need to be sure you are most protected.

RINKs need to rely on the portfolio to provide financial security more than anything else. Of course this is less of an issue if you have a very large, guaranteed-pension income stream coming in each month and, even then, you may have emergency needs for large cash outlays. Also, if you live a long lifetime, most pensions will not increase with the cost of living and inflation will decrease your purchasing power.

Your retirement nest egg needs to be significantly larger than someone with children, since you will have to pay for domestic services and medical services that might otherwise be handled by a child. A large financial net worth is your buffer to maintain your independence and dignity, as you grow older in retirement. Do you want to rely on your nephew for assistance after you get back from the hospital following a minor operation? Maybe you only see him just once a year at your sister's Thanksgiving dinner.

While **"money can't buy you love"**, there are certainly a lot of services you can get people to do for you if you have enough money, and that is the position in which you want to be.

Portfolio Investment Policy

Let me get back to determining your portfolio's overall risk-tolerance level. The amount of risk you are willing to take determines your overall *investment policy*. Your investment policy is your formal declaration of your expectations involving the amount of risk you are willing to take and your expected return from a particular investment strategy.

A good financial advisor will have this discussion with you and have you agree and sign an Investment Policy Statement. This statement will be the understanding you each have on how your investment portfolio should be managed. You should have a formal investment policy written down even if you are managing your own investments. This will help you stay the course during the inevitable market downturns and also keep your expectations cemented in reality.

If you have a very conservative investment policy and the equity markets have a great year and are up 25% and your portfolio is up only 10% this may be as expected. In this instance your conservative strategy is designed more to protect you from market downturns than it is to maximize participation in strong "up" markets. If you desire to have greater growth participation in strong "up" markets then you need to increase your exposure to equities in your investment strategy.

Your overall investment strategy's risk is mainly determined by the split you decide on between Equities and Fixed Income. For example, a very conservative portfolio may contain 100% of its investments in fixed income instruments and a very aggressive portfolio may contain 100% of its investments in equities.

In realty, RINKs should have a mix somewhere between 40% to 80% in equities and the balance in fixed income. Before we understand what these different portfolio strategies have done in the past, let's circle back to some of the reasons why RINKs should take on more or less risk, keeping in mind more risk equates to greater long term returns but more portfolio variations over the short run.

Example of Balanced Strategies

In (Figure 11), I have included some of the balanced strategy returns resulting from model portfolios from Dimensional Fund Advisors (DFA). These results show 4 different strategies from Conservative to Aggressive over a 10 year period ending 12/31/2004.

Please note that these returns are not representative of actual managed portfolios. They are well-diversified balanced portfolios using DFA funds without any expenses, so actual returns if you could duplicate this would be lower. This does not represent actual client returns and I am presenting this here solely to help explain portfolio construction. Having said that, I think it gives you a good representation of how returns vary based on the amount of equity in your portfolio.

You will see that over the 1,3,5 & 10-year period ending 12/31/2004, the Aggressive portfolio had the best returns and the Conservative portfolio had the lowest returns. If you look near the bottom of the Figure 11, you will also see that the annual standard deviation (amount of fluctuation or one way to measure risk or variability) is much higher for the Aggressive portfolio versus all the others.

The Aggressive portfolio had both the highest 12 month return (+48.2%) and the lowest 12 month return (-13.2%), during the 10-year period, confirming the fact that it had the most fluctuation and annual risk. You have to ask yourself if you had a $1 million portfolio invested in the Aggressive portfolio for the 12-month period in which it lost −13.2 % would you be ok with that? That means you would have lost $132,000 and at the end of that 12-month period your portfolio would have dropped to $868,000!

The returns here were over a period of time when both the equity markets and fixed income markets performed very well. The future may be much different from the past.

Forget Rules of Thumb

You can't make critical portfolio design decisions by using *simple rules of thumb*. Please keep in mind that rules of thumb are total nonsense. For example, here's one I read a lot in popular financial magazines: "subtract your age from 100 and that's the percentage of your portfolio that you should have in equities".

I have to agree this is very simple to understand, but it doesn't make much sense since it doesn't take some very important factors into consideration, such as, does the person have a $3,000,000 portfolio and spend only $20,000 a year with a great pension or does the person have a $300,000 portfolio, spend $60,000 a year to live on, and have no pension?

BALANCED STRATEGIES	As of December 31, 2004			
	All Available Data: 1995-2004, Monthly			
	CONSERVATIVE	MODERATE	NORMAL	AGGRESSIVE
EQUITY FIXED INCOME	20.00%	40.00%	60.00%	80.00%
	80.00%	60.00%	40.00%	20.00%
ONE-YEAR MODEL TOTAL RETURN	5.80	9.90	14.10	18.30
THREE-YEAR MODEL ANNUALIZED RETURN (%)	6.70	9.50	12.10	14.80
FIVE-YEAR MODEL ANNUALIZED RETURN (%)	6.20	7.40	3.50	9.50
TEN-YEAR MODEL ANNUALIZED RETURN (%)	7.60	9.20	10.60	12.00
TEN-YEAR MODEL ANNUALIZED STANDARD DEVIATION (%)	2.90	5.50	8.30	11.10
LOWEST ANNUAL MODEL RETURN (%)	2.60 (10/97-9/98)	-25 (4/02-3/03)	-7.9 (4/02-3/03)	-13.2 (4/02-3/03)
HIGHEST ANNUAL MODEL RETURN (%)	13.90 (2/95-1/96)	23.90 (4/03-3/04)	35.60 (4/03-3/04)	48.20 (4/03-3/04)
MODEL GROWTH OF $1 (1995-2004)	2.09	2.09	2.74	3.1

Figure 11

Can one person tolerate a lot of risk while the other can't sleep at night if one monthly brokerage statement shows a loss? I have clients who are over 90 years old and are willing to be very aggressive with their portfolios and short-term losses don't bother them at all. I also have young professional clients who are in their 30's with great incomes and a long term investment horizon but can't tolerate short term market volatilities.

The equity/fixed income split must take into consideration your individual circumstances, your investment personality, and, *especially, your ability to sleep at night.* Forget rules of thumb; they are only good to sell magazines.

Let's say after you have completed some in depth cash flow analysis and financial planning coupled with a discussion of your ability to accept market risk you decide that an investment strategy of 60% equities and 40% fixed income is the appropriate investment policy for you. At this point, if you were working with a good financial advisor your job would be done and it's his job to then construct, maintain and report on the portfolio according to your investment policy. If you are managing the portfolio yourself let me explain what you should consider in constructing your portfolio. Let's define some terms first.

Investing Terms

Let me define some terms that I will be using in this chapter.

Asset class – basically a group of assets (investments) with similar risk and reward characteristics. Cash, debt instruments, real estate and equities are all examples of asset classes. Within a general asset class such as equities there are more specific sub-asset classes such as large-company stocks, small-company stocks, international-large company stocks, and many more.

In constructing a well-balanced diversified portfolio, we need to perform an *Asset Allocation,* which is the process of determining what percentage of assets should be dedicated to which specific asset class.

Before we go further into portfolio construction, I need to address two other topics, which will help in deciding on the investment vehicles to be used in constructing your portfolio. These are the topics of *Active Management and Passive Management.*

Your portfolio can control risk better and you will obtain better long-term rates of return by constructing a portfolio using low cost mutual funds and ETFs. The funds will generally fall into two main categories based on how they are managed, either actively or passively.

Active Management

Active management is the attempt by the management team of the mutual fund to uncover securities the market has either under or overvalued. It is also the attempt to time investment decisions in order to be more heavily invested when the market is rising and less so when the market is falling.

Unlike passive management, active management rests on the assumptions that markets are inefficient. One of the premises upon which this inefficiency is based is the notion that investors are not rational beings and, in fact, inefficiencies develop in the market because investors are irrational. The existence of financial bubbles and market crashes suggests such inefficiencies may exist and active managers attempt to exploit those inefficiencies in order to beat the market on a risk-adjusted basis as measured by a particular index.

Advantages of Active Management

The primary advantage of active management is the potential for higher returns. By taking active "bets" relative to the benchmark, or by assuming more risk, active management offers the potential for investors to realize higher returns relative to market returns. In theory, active management also offers more protection in down markets since the active manager has the ability to raise more cash or invest in more conservative stocks to act as a cushion during market declines and this protection during "down" markets makes up for lower returns than passively managed funds during strong "up" markets.

Disadvantages Of Active Management

One of the main disadvantages of actively managed funds is higher costs and fees. Since most passively-managed funds simply replicate an index, they have very low turnover of investments and therefore, lower trading costs and management fees. An actively-managed fund has much higher costs since it must pay teams of analysts to research stocks, portfolio managers to select stocks, and higher trading costs associated with the higher turnover.

Also, actively-managed funds usually rely on one or two managers' track records of outperforming the market over a certain period of time. What if the manager's stock-picking ability changes or he leaves your fund to take a job at another mutual fund company? These factors can have negative results on your future performance.

In addition, most actively-managed funds are more tax inefficient than passively-managed funds over a long period of time. Of course, this doesn't matter if the fund is in a retirement account, but this *will* reduce your after tax returns when placed in a taxable account.

Passive Management

Passive-management is an investment strategy that mirrors a market index and does not attempt to beat the market. Passive management is the belief in the *efficient market hypothesis*. The efficient market theory is that market prices reflect the knowledge and expectations of all investors. It asserts that any new development is instantaneously priced into a security, thus making it impossible to *consistently* beat the market. No investor has an advantage in predicting a return on a stock price since no one has access to information not already available to everyone else.

Advantages of Passive Management

Passively-managed funds or index funds are market-driven, not driven by an investment manager selecting stocks. They deliver broad, diversified exposure to the market asset class being covered and do not have the problem of some actively-managed funds with manager-style drift. Manager-style drift occurs when a mutual fund manager buys investments that are much different than the stated intention of the fund.

In addition, passively-managed funds have very low expenses, usually 1/5 the expense ratio of an actively-managed fund. This comes from very low overhead, since the fund will just track a particular index and no one is being paid to select stocks. The very low turnover of stocks in the passively-managed fund also makes them much more tax-efficient for use in taxable accounts. This is an additional advantage in high-tax states like New York.

Passively-managed funds are increasingly becoming popular, since much empirical evidence and academic research supports the notion that it is nearly impossible to beat a market portfolio consistently over time after accounting for fees, costs and capital gains taxes.

Disadvantages of Passive Management

Since passive management is a long term buy and hold strategy designed to simply match a particular market's performance, people who have the need to have a short-term winning strategy will be disappointed at times and, therefore, could get discouraged. Another disadvantage is the inability to provide defensive measures during market downturns since the passively-managed fund is always 100% invested so that particular component of your portfolio will fall in line with the overall market it is tracking. With passively-managed strategies, risk is controlled at the portfolio allocation, not the fund level.

So Which Is Better Active or Passive?

In the investment community the debate over which provides better long-term investment returns has been going on for many years. I have read hundreds of studies and articles written by both sides of this debate. Many are very convincing, but lead to opposite conclusions. If you search on the Internet or do any amount of research, you will find enormous amounts of information from both sides of this debate.

You will also find very successful investment managers who have achieved good long-term performance with active investment strategies and you will find many successful money-management firms employing only passively managed strategies.

After years of investing money and managing portfolios for clients, I believe the best approach to portfolio construction for RINKs is to use an intelligent combination of mostly passively-managed funds as a core and supplement the core portfolio with a small amount of actively managed funds when needed.

The passively-managed fund's benefits of low expenses, style consistency and tax efficiency is much too powerful to disregard and automatically increases your odds of better investment returns. I believe the approach you should take is what is being touted as the *core and satellite* or *core and explore* approach.

For most of your equity allocation (the core) you can use passively-managed funds or ETFs and use actively-managed funds (the satellites) when they do something that you can't achieve with a passively managed fund or index. This may be a commodity fund or a hedging type fund, if you believe it makes sense.

On the fixed-income side of your portfolio, the current selection of bond index funds, are limited. I am convinced that a very low-cost, actively-managed bond fund makes good sense and can add value when you are looking at opportunities in specialized bonds such as floating rate bonds, junk bonds and international bonds.

Back To Constructing Your Portfolio

I started the chapter recommending how you should construct an investment portfolio and later I used an example that was 60% in equities and 40% in fixed income. Of course, there are many models of portfolios available that at any given point in time will tell you what funds you should use to make up the mix of investments in your portfolio.

You can research any of the investment websites, go to any brokerage firm, and they will give you their mix of recommended funds to make up a 60/40-investment portfolio. A few things you need to remember is that you must first understand the costs and fees that will be charged to you to implement these model portfolios.

As we discussed in an earlier chapter, using investment vehicles with low fees and expenses goes a long way to increasing your wealth and allowing you to maintain your independence in retirement and that is our constant goal. You also must consider your flexibility to be able to rebalance these investments once combined to make your portfolio.

Many people get into trouble by reading some article about a recommended mix of funds that the author believes will perform well in the future and blindly following that asset allocation. But then, usually, there is no review of the recommended mix in the future. Did the author change his mind in three months? (Keep in mind most of the writers of these articles don't manage money for a living. They are journalists and writers).

While established, pre-canned model portfolios may be fine for someone who doesn't have a good understanding of investments, you will receive the most benefit if your portfolio is custom constructed just for you. A custom portfolio allows you to be tax smart in deciding which investments should be placed in your taxable and tax-deferred accounts.

Consider All Your Investments As One Portfolio

The best way to manage all of your assets in retirement is to view all of your assets as one portfolio and balance your investments in one overall strategy. Since you most likely have several different types of accounts, (taxable, trust, IRA, Roth IRA etc.), you need to first consolidate all of your accounts at one discount broker to make portfolio management easier, as we mentioned in an earlier chapter.

Once you have your investments consolidated and you are viewing all of your assets as one portfolio, only then are you ready to begin to make selections of which investment vehicle should go into what type of account. This is where custom portfolio management can add significant value, since everyone's mix of where his or her different *buckets* of money are will be different.

What I mean by *buckets* is the type of account your investment is in. For example, your total liquid net worth may be $1,000,000 and you have $500,000 in a joint account with your spouse, you have $25,000 in a Roth IRA, and $275,000 in a rollover IRA. Your spouse also has $200,000 in an IRA. Here all of your assets are divided between 4 different buckets that can't be intermixed.

You have combined half your money in a taxable account and half in tax-deferred accounts. In deciding which investment to place in which account you must consider the taxation of the investment. Ideally, you would want to put investments that generate taxable income and short-term gains into your IRAs. In your IRAs the taxes will be deferred until the money is withdrawn, then it is taxed at the regular income tax rates and you receive no benefit from the lower long term capital gains tax rate.

Some investments you should consider for your IRA accounts might be Real Estate Investment Trusts (REITS), junk bond funds, taxable bond funds and activity-managed funds that distribute mostly short-term gains or interest income. Candidates for your taxable joint account would be passively-managed index funds, especially ETFs, or tax-free bonds. Of course, this makes balancing your portfolio much more difficult, but over time you should save a significant amount of money in taxes, especially in states with high income taxes.

The Role of Taxes In Portfolio Construction

You should understand the different way investments are taxed in order to properly balance your portfolio. Interest and short-term gains are taxed at your regular income tax rate, so if you are in a combined state and federal tax bracket of 35%, that is what percentage you will lose to taxes in your taxable joint account. If those same investments were placed in your IRA you are not taxed until you withdraw the money from your IRA, at which time all withdrawals are taxed as regular income.

Currently, long-term capital gains and dividend income are taxable at a lower rate, with the maximum rate being only 15%

federal (you also have your state income tax to pay). It would be to your benefit to take long-term gains in your taxable account. ETFs make good investment vehicles for your taxable account since they have very few taxable distributions and you have a lot of flexibility in improving your after-tax return by controlling when you take profits with ETFs.

Unrealized gains are gains that you have on investments that you won't pay any taxes on until you sell them. It's wonderful to have unrealized gains each year without having part of your profit siphoned off to Uncle Sam. Unrealized long-term gains in your taxable account are better than in your IRA since money coming out of your IRA is taxed at the higher regular tax rate. When you sell and take a long-term profit in your taxable account, you would produce a lower tax.

In addition, if you die with large unrealized gains in your taxable account, the persons inheriting your investments inherit them at the *stepped-up basis*. This means your heirs' new cost basis for the investment is the price of the investment on the day you die, not your cost. If you bought Microsoft for $1 a share and when you die it's worth $100 a share, the person inheriting the stock can immediately turn around and sell it for $100 a share with no capital gains tax due. You don't get the same benefit if the investment is in an IRA. Of course, you don't benefit if you're dead, your heirs do!

Tax Loss Harvesting

You can add additional value to your overall wealth by harvesting losses in your portfolio at the appropriate time. This is called *tax-loss harvesting* and it is the process of reviewing your taxable accounts near the end of the year to determine if you have any positions that currently are trading for less than you paid for them. You would sell the losing positions to capture the tax loss to reduce your taxes for the current year.

If you have a fund in a taxable account (non-IRA) that has gone down since you bought it, you have two choices: do nothing and wait for it to come back up (which is what most folks do, since it requires no action), or swap the fund for a similar fund and realize the loss for income tax purposes. The loss you generate will offset any capital gains you have in that year or, if you have more losses than gains, it will reduce your regular taxable income by up to $3,000. The balance will be carried over to future years to be used against future gains (yes, you will have gains again). In any case, you do not lose the value of your harvested loss.

Tax Loss Example

Let me give you a very simplified example of taking a tax loss. Let's say you have a $10,000 short-term loss, and your combined marginal tax bracket is 36%. That means Uncle Sam picks up $3,600 and your real loss is only $6,400.

Now the law says you cannot buy the same investment within 30 days. But by using Exchange Traded Funds (Ishares, SPDRs, etc.) and similar passively-managed funds, we can immediately exchange one type of fund for one with similar portfolio characteristics, but such is considered a substantially different fund, according to the IRS.

You will make sales in your taxable account, followed by buys, for similar dollar values. In the above example, you paid $10,000 for a mutual fund and since the current value is $6,400 you would sell the fund, take the $6,400 proceeds, and immediately purchase another similar fund. Many good financial advisors do this aggressively for their top clients and you should actively harvest tax losses also. It requires more time and work, and it will also make your accountant think you are a poor investor with many losses, but you will save a lot of money on taxes.

Diversification In Your Portfolio

Diversification is much more than simply not putting all of your eggs in one basket. *Diversification* means the acquisition of a group of assets in which the returns on the assets are not directly related over time. The idea is for you to create a portfolio of assets that are not similarly affected by the same variables over time with the intention of reducing your portfolio's overall risk.

One of the keys to creating a good retirement portfolio is to blend a mix of asset classes, which have low correlations to each other, based on past historic data. Very basically, you do not want all of your investments going up and down at the same time. The blending of low-correlated assets in your portfolio will produce lower portfolio volatility and better compounded returns over time.

Many people mistakenly believe since they have a lot of different investments that they are well diversified but, in fact, I usually find upon examining the portfolio that they have ineffective diversification. Their investments exhibit very similar patterns of performance. What you want to have is effective diversification by combining mutual funds with different patterns of performance over time. You can find correlation data on different asset classes and different mutual funds on the Internet from services such as Morningstar. If you have a desire to learn more about asset class diversification and correlations you can find tons of information on the Internet about this topic.

Lower Volatility

When comparing two portfolios with the same historical average annual return, the one with the lower volatility (up and down movement) in market value will have the higher cumulative rate of return. In the included example (Figure 12), you see two different hypothetical portfolios, the values and return rates are just used for example purposes.

Let's look at this example: both portfolios start out with $100,000. Let's call portfolio #1 Ray's Boring Well-Diversified RINKs Portfolio and portfolio #2 Your Non-Diversified Growth Portfolio.

My portfolio has some bonds, large cap. stocks , small cap. stocks, international stocks and REITs; many different asset

Lower Volatility Results in Higher Compounded Returns

	Year 1	Year 2	Year 3
	10%	10%	10%
1 $100,000	$110,000	$121,000	$133,100
	20%	-10%	20%
2 $100,000	$120,000	$108,000	$129,600

Both portfolios have a 10% average annual rate of return.

Figure 12

classes with low correlations to each other. Your #2 portfolio is heavily weighted with investments that are mostly in U.S. Large Company Stocks.

Year one of our example was a very good year for U.S. Large Company Stocks and your portfolio was up 20% while I had some U.S. Large Company Stocks, I also had other asset classes that didn't do so well in year one, so my portfolio was up only 10%. Your portfolio's performance was double mine after the first year. Your chest is puffed up with pride at being such a smart investor and you believe I'm a dope for investing in the other assets that didn't do so well.

Year two was not a good year for U.S. Large Company Stocks and portfolio #2 lost 10%. While my portfolio #1 also had some U.S. Large Company Stocks that went down, some of my other asset classes did very well that year, such as REITs, Small Value Stocks and Bonds, so my overall return was again up 10%. Year 2, I beat you.

Year three was very kind once again to U.S. Large Company Stocks and your portfolio #2 again gained 20% while my diversified portfolio #1 only gained 10%.

Two out of the three years your portfolio's gain was double the gain of my portfolio (year 1 & year 3) but look who ended up with more money! The *average return rate* of both of these portfolios is the same 10% over the three year period but **portfolio #1 ends up with more money due to having lower overall volatility.** Lower overall portfolio volatility will produce higher long-term compounded returns.

What Goes Into Your Portfolio?

When constructing your portfolio, whether it is 60% Equities and 40% Fixed Income or some other combination, you need to consider all of the issues we spoke about in this chapter just as a starting point. I can't give you an actual recommendation of which funds to put into your portfolio and at what percentages, since I believe this will vary based not only on your Investment Policy but also current economic conditions.

Current market valuations of the different asset classes must come into play when deciding which asset class to invest in and at what percentage of that asset class. At a certain point in time, REITS may look extremely inexpensive based on past valuations, so you may want 6% of your portfolio in REITS. At a different point in time, REITS may have had a five-year run of outperforming other asset classes and their valuations are now very expensive based on past valuations, so it may then be prudent to lower or eliminate REITS from your portfolio. These portfolio decisions require you to perform asset class valuation research and stay abreast of current economic conditions.

Portfolio Rebalancing

In building your portfolio, your first and most important step is creating an appropriate asset allocation mix. Maintaining that allocation is equally important and this is where *portfolio rebalancing* comes into play. Portfolio rebalancing is the means of buying and selling within your portfolio to maintain your overall desired asset-allocation mix.

Portfolio rebalancing should be done on a regular basis, which could be four times a year or just once a year. I have found that quarterly portfolio reviews and rebalancing is a good interval for maintaining a desired portfolio mix. The idea of portfolio rebalancing is to sell off assets that have gone up a lot and are now a higher percentage of your desired amount and to purchase assets that have gone down or are now a lower percentage of your desired amount.

For example, if your desired asset allocation is to have 20% in U.S. Large Co. core allocation and 15% in U.S. Small Co. core allocation and, after a good run by small company stocks, they now comprise 20% of your portfolio, you would sell off 5% of the small co. stocks and buy more of whatever asset classes were below your desired percentage.

The reason that most people don't do this is that it requires you to sell winners and turn around and perhaps buy losers. This is psychologically not palatable for most people who will continue to let their winners run. The disciplined strategy of regular rebalancing forces you to *sell high and buy low.* Isn't that what investing is all about?

Rebalancing Reduces Risk

The other benefit of disciplined regular rebalancing is that you lower the risk of your overall portfolio by limiting your exposure to one asset class. Remember, we diversify investments to limit our overall portfolio volatility and risk. If you don't rebalance you will end up with one asset class dominating your portfolio and if that asset class drops your overall returns will be hurt.

If you started out in the 1990s with a well- diversified, balanced portfolio and never rebalanced, by the year 2000 you could have had as much as 50% of your portfolio in large company growth stocks. In the following three years when large company growth stocks crashed, your retirement portfolio would have suffered greatly, so much so that your retirement lifestyle would have had to be dramatically lowered.

From interviewing prospective clients this is exactly what some retirees allowed to happen to their portfolios and their retirement. Don't let this happen to you, ***rebalance!***

More on Rebalancing

You need to be tax smart when rebalancing. You must try to minimize capital gains taxes when you rebalance. In many cases you can achieve this by doing most of the rebalancing in your IRA or tax-deferred accounts.

If you must rebalance in a taxable account try to wait until you own the position for one year so the gain will be at the lower long-term capital gains rate. You may also rebalance the portfolio by directing new incoming money to the underweighted asset classes, therefore increasing their percentage in your mix. Just remember that it is better to pay some tax than to have a portfolio that is not well balanced.

Another reason to rebalance is if you decide to make a tactical change to your portfolio's asset allocation. As mentioned above, if you no longer want to include REITS in your asset allocation and decide to sell off that position, you must now recalculate your overall percentages of the other asset classes and determine where to invest the REIT money.

In addition to your regular quarterly portfolio review and rebalancing, there usually are other causes during the year that will force you to make some changes and rebalance your portfolio. In (Figure 13a), I have included a rebalancing report from my portfolio management software. This report shows how much the client is off from her desired portfolio allocation according to her Investment Policy Statement.

Portfolio Rebalancing
Normal 60%EQ 40%FI

Description	Weight	Target Percent	Percent Variance	Current Value	Target Value	Dollar Variance
Large Co.	28.0%	25.0%	-3.0	478,822.65	427,746.43	-51,076.23
Small Co.	10.5%	9.0%	-1.5	180,041.56	153,988.71	-26,052.85
REITS/Real Estate	12.9%	14.0%	1.1	221,033.75	239,538.00	18,504.25
International	14.5%	14.0%	-0.5	247,281.48	239,538.00	-7,743.48
Commodity Futures	3.0%	5.0%	2.0	51,942.42	85,549.29	33,606.87
Fixed Inc.	27.2%	33.0%	5.8	465,060.70	564,625.28	99,564.58
Cash	3.9%	0.0%	-3.9	66,803.14	0.00	-66,803.14
	100.0%	100.0%		$1,710,985.70	$1,710,985.70	

Figure 13a

Chapter Summary

You need a properly managed, well-diversified portfolio in order to ensure you have enough money during your long retirement. When creating your portfolio, you first must understand your risk tolerance since this will dictate your Investment Policy or your mix between equities and fixed income. You should also ignore "rules of thumb" when investing and instead, take into account your own unique situation.

Two main styles of investing are active and passive management. While active management tries to beat the market each year, passive management tries to capture the market's overall return. I believe that your portfolio should primarily be invested in passively managed investments since they have low expenses and are very tax-efficient.

You should view all of your brokerage accounts as one large portfolio. When managing your portfolio you have to be aware of taxes. By realizing tax loss harvesting and proper placement of your investments, you can gain additional wealth from tax savings.

The main reason for having a diversified portfolio of non-correlated assets is to lower your portfolio's overall volatility. Lower portfolio volatility leads to higher long-term compounded returns. You must regularly rebalance your portfolio in order to keep your investments in balance and reduce the risk to your portfolio. There are many reasons to rebalance your portfolio during the year, and you should try to be tax smart when you perform your rebalancing.

8) Smart Retirement Portfolio Distributions

That's enough, Charlie. Don't show me any more figures; I've got the smell of the thing now.

-Henry Ford

You worked hard, sacrificed your entire working life and saved for your future retirement and now it's here. Congratulations! Now you have to get used to the idea that, instead of saving money every month into your brokerage account, you will be taking money out each month on which to live.

Some people have a very difficult time with the idea that they now must reverse course and begin to withdraw from their portfolio. They do everything possible to delay it but, at some point, they should be drawing down their assets. You're a RINK! You don't have to worry about leaving your hard-earned money to grandkids. This was the point of all of that saving and sacrificing. Now you should get comfortable with the idea of enjoying your money. Of course, the drawdown or distributions from your nest egg has to be accomplished in an intelligent manner so that you do not run out of money while you are still alive.

The question you should ask is how much can I afford to spend each month? If you spend too much when you first retire you may not have enough money later in your retirement when you may need it most for additional health care costs and extra services. On the other hand, if you sacrifice and deprive yourself of spending, then you will leave more to your estate and perhaps pay more estate taxes, and that is not your goal as a RINK. You may need to ensure that your withdrawals increase each year to keep up with inflation, our enemy #1.

Unexpected Expenses Always Come?

Since you want to remain independent your entire life, making the determination of how much you can safely withdraw each month in early retirement is very important. If you are overly optimistic in your expectations on the returns you will achieve from your investments and start off with a very high initial withdrawal rate, you may end up being financially helpless the rest of your life.

Many events can happen that could cause you to go over your planned budget if you are not careful: Your car gets stolen, you need expensive dental or medical care that you must pay out of pocket, you fall and break your leg and need to have someone to cook, bath and help you get dressed. Remember, as a RINK you will have to pay for this assistance from a service provider, possibly a geriatric care manager, since you don't have a dedicated child to help you.

If you own your home you already know how unexpected expenses can pop up: your roof needs replacing, your heating system fails in the middle of winter, that tree you planted when you first bought your home didn't last as long as you and now has to be taken down. As a retiree, depending on your health and physical condition, some of the things you may have done yourself in the past now have to be done by someone else and at a high service cost. Especially since most of these unplanned expenses must be done as an emergency when you will be charged the most for the service.

Do It All Yourself?

I have one client who is in her eighties and could well afford to pay a lawn service to cut her grass but she insists on doing it herself with a gas powered push mower. She doesn't have the strength to pull start her lawnmower so she waits for the mailman to come by to start it for her. She cuts her own lawn because she is healthy enough to do it and she believes it keeps her in good physical shape. She asks, "Ray why do all those silly people walk around the mall to get exercise when they could do chores around the house, save money and stay in shape?"

Now you may not want to or be capable of mowing your own lawn when you are in your eighties. As I tell my clients when we do retirement planning, when you retire we have to plan for higher expenses since in most cases the surprises that happen later in life usually cost you money and drain your portfolio. You can't expect to have a surprise that will increase your wealth, that is, unless you win the lottery or inherit some money!

Use Your Retirement Projections

Of course you can make your monthly budget so low that withdrawals from your investments are just a very tiny percentage of your total assets to ensure you will never run out of money. This will allow for bad years from the stock market or bad economic times, but, after saving and deferring pleasures while you were younger, do you really want to live like a college student pinching pennies in retirement? I don't think so. Remember, your goal is not to leave a large estate to your heirs or taxes to the government.

As we covered in the chapters on retirement planning, the best way to determine a safe monthly withdrawal rate from your investments is by doing a comprehensive retirement analysis using a good cash-flow driven financial planning software program.

The planning software allows you to accurately and easily see the interplay of monthly expenses, return on investment and inflation.

To try to do these calculations manually would be too difficult and time consuming. I have seen some very good retirement planning books that go into great detail with manual calculations, pension factor tables, and complex formulas to help you make the calculations by hand with just a regular calculator. While this material is very informative, I don't think most retirees have the mathematical skill, time or desire to do this by hand. Even if they did, I think the chances of making an error are extremely high.

I would compare it to doing a complicated income tax return. If you ever tried to calculate or understand all of the components that go into determining your AMT (alternative minimum tax) you will know what I mean. If you use a good tax preparation software program it will make all of the interrelated calculations for you instantly and accurately. Of course, with any software program you need to understand the limitations of the program and you still have to know what you are doing in order to use it accurately and properly.

How To Take Your Money

Having completed your retirement projections and determined how much money you need to live on each month, you now need to decide how to take it and which of your brokerage accounts to take it from. If you are just entering retirement, this is a little more involved than what you might think. While working, you were used to handling your budget in a certain way, but now, while the expenses are still being withdrawn from your checking account, your paycheck is no longer being automatically deposited. Even if you have been retired for some time, I'm going to suggest a better way of handling your monthly money and from where you should be taking it.

In retirement, you should be aware that taxes are the primary determinate of where you should be taking your money from each month for living expenses. More than likely, you have several buckets in which your money is currently residing: money in retirement plans (401k, 403b, IRAs, SEPS etc); money in investments that have taxable gains if you sell them; and money on which taxes have already been paid, such as CDs and savings accounts.

The money that you need to withdraw each month from your portfolio should come from your taxable or non-retirement money first. You should try to postpone taking money from your retirement accounts as long as possible in most cases. There may be times when you might consider taking small yearly withdrawals from an IRA before you have to and I'll discuss this later.

Total Return Investing

Unfortunately, many people enter retirement believing the old-fashioned idea that you can live on the interest and dividends from your portfolio and never need to touch the principal. If you think this way you need to better understand portfolio management in order to be sure you have enough money in retirement.

As a RINK, you need to ensure that you have enough growth in your retirement nest egg to pay for the extra services we discussed earlier and you can't do that by living off interest and dividends only; you need to invest for *total return*.

Total return investing means if you retire in your sixties (and for many people even into your late seventies), you should have at least 40% - 60% of your portfolio invested in equities. (I would say 40% at a minimum). A higher percentage of equities can be supported by your individual time horizon, objective and risk tolerance. Bonds alone will not maintain your standard of living above inflation and certainly won't help you build the larger nest egg needed for emergencies.

You may feel that you can't take that kind of risk in retirement but you also have the greater risk of running out of money if you live long enough due to the effects of inflation. Let's say you have part of your money in equities (stocks, etc.) and part in fixed income (CDs, bonds). Where do you take your money from each month?

Well, if you only took interest and dividends from your portfolio, you most likely would not have enough to live on since it's only a small portion of your entire nest egg. You should invest your portfolio for balanced total return and take whatever amount you need each month according to the retirement analysis and projections we discussed earlier.

Tax Smart Withdrawals

When we discussed portfolio construction I suggested that the placement of where you put different investments was mostly driven by income tax considerations. For example, high yielding taxable investments, corporate bonds, and REITS would be best sheltered from income taxes if placed in your IRAs, and tax-efficient index funds and individual stocks would be best placed in your taxable brokerage account.

Of course, it depends on what percentages of your total assets are in taxable accounts versus tax-deferred accounts. In most cases, you may also end up with some fixed income investments in your taxable brokerage accounts and some equities in your tax-deferred or IRA accounts. Sorry; the more accounts you have, the more complicated managing your money becomes, especially when you have to rebalance the asset classes.

Let's assume you have enough money in your taxable account and in your taxable account you have investments that have appreciated. If you sold these appreciated assets you will pay taxes on them but you also should have some investments that have very little gains, perhaps in a short-term bond fund. You should take your monthly withdrawals from the place that causes the least amount of tax when you take it.

This way, you keep more of the money in your account earning for you and Uncle Sam gets less. The place that would generate the least amount of taxes would be from your taxable account and the first investment to liquidate to provide that monthly withdrawal would be anything that doesn't have a taxable gain when sold.

How To Make Withdrawals

In actual practice, this is how I do it for our clients and it should work well for you. Let's say, for example, after the initial planning and budget analysis, we determine that you need $5,000 a month in addition to your social security. We would then set up an automatic transfer to your checking account each month.

Basically, the brokerage firm will move $5,000 a month automatically each month from your taxable brokerage account to your bank checking account where you have your social security check deposited. This would be the checking account where you pay all of your regular monthly bills. You choose the day of the month you want the money to arrive. It is very reliable, and once set up, I have never seen a missed deposit. It works better if you are having the money transferred to your bank checking account from only one brokerage account.

I usually ensure that 3 to 6 months of your monthly withdrawals are always kept in cash in your brokerage money market account so that it will be available for your transfer each month. You might wonder, where does this money come from? Well, since your entire portfolio of all of your accounts is managed for total return, the cash needed comes from two sources.

One is dividends and interest on investments in that taxable account flowing automatically each month into your money market sweep account where it collects some interest while waiting to be transferred to your bank. The other way I generate the cash needed is during our quarterly portfolio review and rebalancing, as I review all of your investments, I will sell something in that taxable account to provide enough cash for the next 3-6 months.

Of course, what I sell helps keep your portfolio mix in line with your overall investment strategy and generates the least amount of tax. Usually, because a portion of your account will be in short term bonds, there will be no taxable gain upon the sale or, if we do have to sell something with a gain, we look for the smallest gain that is taxed at the lower long-term income tax rate, currently just 15% on the federal level.

UNIFORM LIFETIME TABLE

Age of IRA Owner or Plan Participant	Life Expectancy (in years)	Age of IRA Owner or Plan Participant	Life Expectancy (in years)
70	27.4	93	9.6
71	26.5	94	9.1
72	25.6	95	8.6
73	24.7	96	8.1
74	23.8	97	7.6
75	22.9	98	7.1
76	22.0	99	6.7
77	21.2	100	6.3
78	20.3	101	5.9
79	19.5	102	5.5
80	18.7	103	5.2
81	17.9	104	4.9
82	17.1	105	4.5
83	16.3	106	4.2
84	15.5	107	3.9
85	14.8	108	3.7
86	14.1	109	3.4
87	13.4	110	3.1
88	12.7	111	2.9
89	12.0	112	2.6
90	11.4	113	2.4
91	10.8	114	2.1
92	10.2	115+	1.9

Figure 13b

Here is the priority order list, which should be followed when raising cash for your monthly withdrawals.

Priority of Monthly Withdrawals

Taxable Brokerage Account
1) Dividends & Interest (taxable & tax free).
2) Sale of Investments with No Gains.
3) Sale of Investments with Long Term Gains.
4) Sale of Investments with Short Term Gains.

IRA Brokerage Account
1) If not 70.5, do not withdraw.
2) If 70.5, take only required RMD & transfer to taxable brokerage account once a year.

Dividends, interest (either from taxable bonds or tax free bonds) and investment sales proceeds flow to the taxable brokerage accounts' money market sweep fund. Keep 3-6 months of cash in the money market fund and each month automatic transfers go into your household checking account for your normal expenses. The following chart shows the flow of getting your money from your IRA to your personal checking account.

Traditional IRA Account
Once a year RMD transfer to Taxable Account
If over 70.5 years old

l
l

Taxable Brokerage Account
Monthly automatic transfers to bank checking

l
l

Bank Checking Account
Used for normal monthly household bills

Keep Monthly Expenses Separate

Some people like to write checks directly from their brokerage account but I don't think this is a good idea for several reasons. I believe, psychologically, it is important to separate your retirement portfolio/nest egg (which is the engine to generate your future withdrawals) from your household budget.

I have found that keeping your household budget separate from your retirement investments helps instill with clarity a better sense of budget and helps control what you spend. Some people tend to want to write checks whenever they see money in their brokerage account and then their retirement nest egg becomes a piggy bank for any instant gratification need and takes them off track from all of the planning that they did.

Your Checking Account Is A Fuel Gauge

It is better to keep say, $25,000 (or whatever amount allows you to feel comfortable) in your checking account for your monthly bills as a buffer. Some months your expenses will be higher and some months they will be lower, but you have your regular automatic monthly deposits, which feed your checking account on a systematic basis.

This serves another purpose, especially when you first retire. I tell clients that no matter how much you try to estimate your expenses in retirement you won't really know your cash flow needs until living in this new retirement for 6 –12 months. This is especially true if you sell your home and move to another state. The buffer money in your checking account acts like your fuel gauge. If after 6 months the initial $25,000 is down to $5,000, then you know you are spending more than what was initially budgeted in the projections and you need to revisit your expenses.

Now you have to decide: did you use the extra money for one-time expenses to set up a new home, or is it just that you find yourself spending more money than initially estimated? If it's a one- time expense, then you take a lump sum, say $20,000, from your nest egg to replenish your buffer checking account back up to $25,000.

However, if it appears to be ongoing expenses, then you need to increase your money withdrawal from your portfolio and revaluate the long-term impact of these increased withdrawals. If, on the other hand, after 6 months you find yourself with $40,000 in your checking account, then you should consider lowering your automatic withdrawals since your money will earn more in the portfolio than in the checking account.

RMD Withdrawals From IRAs

As we discussed, you want to generally withdraw money from the place where it will generate the least amount of tax, but if you are over 70.5 years old then you must start taking *required minimum distributions* (RMD) from your IRA and other tax-deferred plans.

The amount required to be withdrawn is based on the IRS table, (Figure 13b), and the balance of all of your tax-deferred accounts as of Dec 31 of the previous year. If you are subject to RMD, then you must take this minimum amount each year and you will pay 100% regular income tax on the full amount. You should not take any more than required if you have other money to draw on so that you can continue to defer the taxes as long as possible.

You may want to have monthly withdrawals based on your RMD automatically transferred to your checking account each month, or sometimes it's just easier to have your monthly withdrawal taken from your taxable account and just once a year have a lump sum transfer of your RMD directly from your IRA brokerage account to your taxable brokerage account.

I find this system easier for budgeting since the amount you need to withdraw each month to live on is rarely the same as you are required to take from your IRA. You also have to consult with your tax preparer to determine if you should have taxes withheld from this monthly RMD amount or just pay the taxes when you complete your income tax return.

401k & 403b Rollover

Since we are discussing IRAs, now might be a good time to discuss whether you should roll your 401k or 403b plan over into an IRA or leave it in your company's plan. In most cases it is much better to move your money out of your company plan and into an IRA. There are many factors to consider here. I'll try to address some of the main ones.

Disadvantages of IRA Rollover

You may want to consider leaving your money in your 401k plan for some of the following reasons:

Your company has excellent investment options with low institutional expenses. These may be lower than if you purchased the same funds retail (in most cases the company plan funds have high expenses.)

Some companies may offer the ability to annuitize part of the 401k value at competitive prices paying you an income stream for life (before you do this understand how it fits into your overall investment strategy).

If you need to withdraw the money, you will not be subject to the 10% penalty starting at the age of 55 whereas, if you had rolled it over into an IRA, you would have to wait until you are 59.5 before you won't incur the 10% penalty. (There is a way around the 10% penalty prior to age 59.5 in an IRA by using the IRS code 72(t))

Advantages of IRA Rollover

You can move the money to any brokerage firm or bank that you desire and have an almost unlimited selection of investments to choose to invest within your IRA brokerage account.

It's more favorable to beneficiaries. A drawback to leaving your money in the company plan is that after your death, a spouse is the only beneficiary who can roll the money over into a tax- protected IRA. Companies may have few tax- friendly policies regarding payouts to beneficiaries other than a spouse and, by law, can limit the payout to 5 years and then the tax benefits are lost.

You create the ability to expand the types of investments you can invest in. When you leave the money in the company plan you are saddled with the few investment options they offer. This could hurt your long-term returns since most plan options have high expenses and poorly performing funds.

You have the ability to use the IRA as a tool in your asset allocation to save income taxes by being able to put certain tax-inefficient investments in your IRA, which may not otherwise be available in your company plan. These investments may include REITS, commodity futures funds and junk bonds.

If you have your money professionally managed, you give your advisor much more flexibility in helping you save taxes when there is a large IRA to make tax-deferred trades.

You can avoid the 10% penalty on IRA withdrawals if you are younger than 59.5 by using 72(t). It requires fixed withdrawals for a certain number of years, (explaining how 72(t) works is too complicated for this book, discuss this with your advisor).

Having your money in an IRA is also much better for estate planning. While this may not be a major concern to you as a RINK, it is important if there is someone other than Uncle Sam that you would rather benefit from the proceeds of your IRA upon your death. When you die, the money in your IRA flows according to the beneficiary statement you have on file with the brokerage firm, not your will. Be sure to keep your beneficiary statement current, otherwise, someone may inherit your IRA that is no longer your desired beneficiary.

The laws involving inheriting IRAs are very complicated. Your beneficiaries have more options in stretching the time they have to withdraw money from the inherited IRA than if you left the money in your 401k or 403b plan. The estate- planning benefits of an IRA is one of the main reasons most people will roll their money out of a 401k or 403b plan into an IRA.

You no longer have to deal with your old employer. If your old company goes out of business you will have a hard time getting your money from your old plan even if the 401k plan is held by a large brokerage firm.

You have the opportunity to convert your rollover IRA money to a Roth IRA if you so desire.

Consolidating all of your IRAs into one brokerage account makes taking your RMD much less complicated when you turn 70.5

Quicker access to your money for emergencies. You have the possibility of taking money out of an IRA and putting it back within 60 days without penalty.

Using NUA For Your Company Stock

There are some other issues that involve your own company stock in your 401k plan. You might benefit from something called *NUA, net unrealized appreciation.* This is a way to take your own company stock out of your 401k plan, and pay the tax immediately on your cost basis of the stock but not on the appreciation of the stock. The tax on the gain of the stock won't have to be paid until you sell it, when it will be taxed at the more favorable long-term capital gains rate, currently only 15%.

You will have to make a careful evaluation if it makes sense to use NUA. It could have some benefits if you really want to keep the stock forever and you don't already have too much invested in your company's stock. If you keep it forever and eventually die with the stock, your heirs will get the step up in cost basis and they could immediately sell it and may pay no capital gains tax.

The evaluation of whether you should take stock out of your plan via NUA or roll it over into an IRA most likely will require the help of a professional advisor or tax preparer, since it is complicated and your company must code the distribution correctly.

Take IRA Withdrawals Early?

Previously, I mentioned there might be a situation where, while you don't need the money, it would make sense to take withdrawals early and pay taxes on your IRA prior to age 70.5. This strategy makes sense if you are currently in a low- tax bracket and you expect to be in a higher tax bracket when you start taking RMD. Since you may be in a higher tax bracket when you reach 70.5 you would benefit by taking some money out now and paying the taxes on it.

Let me explain by an example. I have a client who is 65 years old with $2,000,000 in an IRA and $2,000,000 in his taxable accounts. The client has a balanced portfolio, with his investments positioned in the proper accounts to minimize income taxes. This is especially important for our New York clients who pay high taxes.

Since his investments are positioned to reduce income taxes, this client is currently in a very low tax bracket although he has $4,000,000 in investments. The reason his income taxes are low is that we position tax-exempt bonds and passively-managed tax-efficient ETF indexes in his taxable account and put the tax-inefficient investments such as Real Estate funds, commodities, emerging market debt, etc. in his IRAs.

Currently this client is only in the 15% federal income tax bracket since his only income is $20,000 a year from social security and some dividends from the index funds. He is not 70.5 so he is not required to take any money from his IRA yet, but we do take some. Why? If his $2,000,000 in his IRA only grows at 5% a year he will have approximately $2,600,000 when he must start taking his required minimum distributions (RMD) at age 70.5.

His RMD will be approximately $95,000 according to the current IRS tables ($2,600,000/27.4 years). So this client will be in a much higher income tax bracket when he is 70.5 than he is now, since he will have $95,000 more in taxable income. This will push him from the 15% federal tax bracket to the 28% federal tax bracket (at today's tax rates). Of course, you also have to add state income tax, which may add another 7% or so.

Here we try to draw down an amount of his IRA that will keep him from going into the next tax bracket each year until he is 70.5. He also benefits since, in New York, you are not taxed on the first $20,000 of pension money coming in once you turn 59 ½ and IRA withdrawals fall into this category. If we take out $20,000 each year from his IRA he pays no New York tax on the money, only 15% federal tax. Of course, your situation may be different and you should have a good tax preparation program to help determine how much is just the right amount.

Being smart about portfolio positioning and IRA withdrawing can save you a lot of tax money and help make your portfolio last longer, which will allow you to spend more in your retirement. We have many clients with large investment portfolios who pay very little income tax each year because of intelligent planning. If you pay attention to income taxes and implement strategies to save taxes, you will also enjoy more spending money in your retirement.

Early IRA Roth Conversions

A variation on the above strategy is if you want to pay the taxes early at the lower income tax bracket but still want to keep your money in a tax-deferred vehicle. As long as your modified adjusted gross income is below $100,000 in the year of conversion you can convert the money in your traditional IRA into a Roth IRA, pay the income tax on the money, and let it continue to grow in the Roth IRA tax-deferred.

You would consider doing this if you don't expect to need this money and, by placing it in the Roth IRA, it is even more beneficial than a regular IRA since you never have to pay taxes on the money when you withdraw it (as long as it's in the Roth 5 years) and you are not forced to withdraw your money from the Roth IRA ever. When you die, your beneficiaries have to start withdrawals.

Chapter Summary

First, you need to determine your required portfolio monthly withdrawals using the projections and assumptions from your retirement planning. Next, it would be a good idea to set up a buffer amount of money in your checking account from which you will pay your normal bills, using the checking account as your fuel gauge.

The checking account should be fed each month with automatic withdrawals from your long-term investment portfolio. These withdrawals should be taken from the brokerage accounts that will generate the least amount of taxes as possible. You should tap your taxable accounts first and your tax deferred accounts such as IRAs last so you can continue to defer taxes as long as possible.

For most people, the benefits of rolling your 401k or 403b plan into an IRA are overwhelming, but there might be certain situations where it would be better to leave your money in the company plan or take your company stock out using the NUA, (net unrealized appreciation).

You also might consider taking some of your money from your IRA early and paying the taxes on it if you expect to be in a higher tax bracket once you turn 70.5. A smart variation of this strategy is to convert part of your traditional IRA each year into a Roth IRA.

9) Finding & Working With A Trusted Financial Advisor

Nothing astonishes men so much as
common sense and plain dealing.
-Ralph Waldo Emerson

As a RINK I believe it is critically important to the management of your life's affairs for you to develop a professional relationship with a trusted advisor early in your retirement, ideally 5 years or so before you retire. Your trusted advisor will help you navigate through the ever-changing complexities of the financial environment, allowing you to enjoy your retirement without constant worry about money decisions.

Your trusted financial advisor is a very important cornerstone to the success of your overall retirement planning and should be the quarterback on your *$Team* of advisors. But do you really need an advisor? Who should you turn to and how can you find someone that you can trust? I'll try to answer some of these questions in this chapter.

The skeptics will say, "Hey Ray! Of course you think I need a financial advisor! That's how you make your living!" That is true, and, of course, you have to decide for yourself, but I certainly can't be everyone's financial advisor. My firm is small and we intentionally limit the number of clients we work with so that we can provide a high level of personal service to our clients.

The advice I'm giving in this chapter will help you find someone that I believe you will benefit from over the years. Since as a RINK you have no children to provide assistance in your golden years, you need to have someone in your corner when you need help. You are not going to get that commitment of caring if you just walk into a brokerage house when you have a problem.

Since you are reading this book, I'm assuming that you have at least $500,000 or more of liquid net worth besides your home and you don't have any children that can help give you guidance as you get older when, maybe, you're not as on top of things as you once were. Or maybe you just want to enjoy retirement and not have to worry about the day-to-day financial decisions. To me, you are a prime candidate for a trusted financial advisor and you need to develop the relationship early while, you are still younger, say mid-50s on up.

Why Start Working With Someone Early?

While I believe most people would benefit from working with a good financial advisor all during their working years, it is more critical as you get nearer retirement since you now have accumulated significant wealth and financial mistakes become more crippling to your successful retirement.

You need to start your search early for a good advisor because *it is very difficult to find someone who is experienced, technically competent and will be objective, always putting your best interest first.* Unfortunately, after a few years, you may find out that the situation isn't working well and you will have to begin your search over until you locate an advisor that is right for you.

Preferably, you don't want to wait until you are 80 years old to begin the relationship because, as a RINK, as you get further into retirement you will come to rely more and more on your financial advisor. Of course if you are already retired and need to find someone new, you need to start looking *now*.

Even with the information you read in this chapter, getting referrals from others, and conducting your own interviews, the person you initially choose may not turn out to be a good fit for your personality. You could be into the relationship 2 – 3 years before you determine you need to switch and work with someone else and so the clock is ticking.

From my experience, it may take anywhere from 2-5 years for you to determine if your advisor is a trusted advisor. Sometimes you need to see how the advisor handles your anxieties during stressful times, such as the stock market drop following the World Trade Center terrorist attack. Many people found out that their advisor wasn't so great when the stock market dropped during 2000-2003.

What Is A *Trusted Advisor?*

I don't use the term trusted advisor lightly. I became a CERTIFIED FINANCIAL PLANNER™ practitioner in 1989. I have been the Vice President of Ethics for the Long Island chapter of the Financial Planners Association (FPA) for several years and currently I am the chapter President with more than 575 members.

Over the years I have attended many financial planning conferences, seminars and have read thousands of trade journal articles on the business of financial advice. I feel pretty comfortable that I understand how the different people in this business operate. There are only a minor number of professionals who call themselves a financial advisor who I would consider calling a trusted advisor.

To me, a good trusted financial advisor is someone who helps you determine your life goals, helps you achieve those goals by ongoing monitoring and management of your financial affairs, and does this in an objective, caring manner, putting your interests first. The advisor should act as a *fiduciary*; you will know exactly how much you are paying for his services and the advisor should not be compensated by any other party except you. If the advisor makes recommendations for you to work with other professionals there should not be any form of referral fees or kickbacks to the advisor.

A good trusted advisor should have a well-rounded knowledge of financial planning issues and should refer you to the proper professional when something is beyond his expertise. Ideally, the advisor will have the wisdom and experience that can only come from working with other clients like you.

You Can Call Yourself A Financial Advisor

Unfortunately, anyone can have some business cards printed up, take an ad in the yellow pages and call himself a financial advisor. These days it is getting more difficult to understand the differences between all of the individuals looking for your business.

You have the large brokerage firms calling their brokers financial advisors, insurance salesmen, bank employees, tax preparers, accountants and even some lawyers all presenting themselves as financial advisors. There are no laws governing who can pass themselves off as competent professionals. This just makes your search even more difficult and wrought with pitfalls. The consequences to you of working with the wrong professional could be ruinous to your financial health.

Follow The Money

As Deep Throat was alleged to have said during the Watergate crisis, "follow the money". Understanding how a financial person is paid is a very powerful tool in helping you find an objective advisor. There is a lot of money to be made in the financial services business selling products and all of that money will end up coming out of your pocket.

You need to be sure that the service you are receiving is reflected in the fee/commission that you will be paying. You need to know and understand how the financial advisor is being paid. If he tells you that you aren't paying him anything, run for the door.

I would like to make two important points. One is that in any form of advisor compensation, if the advisor is unethical, there is the potential for abuse. The form of compensation alone doesn't make one person more ethical than another. The other point that I would like to make is, if you are currently working with someone and have been for many years and he has been a good advisor to you, you certainly wouldn't change because of the way he is being paid.

Certainly there are many variations of compensation for financial professionals working with individuals. The three main forms that you will find are *Commissions, Fee-based and Fee-only.* I will discuss these different forms of compensation.

Commission-Only Advisors

Commission only advisors make all, or the majority, of their income from commissions on selling financial products. People who work on commissions get paid by the company that produces the product and not directly by you. This is the key to the potential conflict of interest. Some of the advisors who get paid on commissions are stockbrokers, mutual fund salespeople and almost all insurance salespeople.

The commission form of compensation is the least desirable for you as a successful RINK since, in many cases, the amount of compensation is never disclosed to you. How can you be sure that you are being offered the product that is best for your situation and not simply the one which provides the largest commissions to the salesperson?

One of the major drawbacks that you will have working with a commission based advisor is that the product you are sold may limit your portfolio management flexibility. In earlier chapters I discussed portfolio management and the importance of having a brokerage account that has a platform that allows you to invest in thousands of mutual funds.

In the commission-based mutual fund world, if you buy a large company growth fund with a sales load today from one company and next year you want to switch to a real estate fund, you will most likely have to stay within that same fund company family. This severely limits your options. What if that fund company has a great large company growth fund but a lousy real estate fund?

A commission based advisor is best for individuals with smaller amounts of assets since they won't have enough money to make it profitable to work with a Fee-Only advisor. For individuals with modest assets working with a good commission based advisor may be their only option in receiving helpful financial advice. As long as the advisor explains that the commission compensates him for all of the other financial advice the client can expect to receive during the year. You should also clearly understand how he is compensated so there will be no misunderstanding or mistaken assumptions.

Fee-based Advisor

A Fee-based advisor will generally charge a fee but may also collect commissions on products that you buy. Many times this is someone who started working on commissions only and is transitioning his business to being compensated more by fees. It is difficult for the advisor to totally drop his commission business because of the revenue it provides him.

Also, some advisors may charge a fee based on managing your investment portfolio like a Fee-Only advisor but he also has the ability to sell you insurance products that are sold by commissions only advisors. I know of some very good advisors who work with a wide variety of clients and for their clients with fewer assets, they offer commission based products while, for the clients with greater assets, they will work on a fee basis.

As with all forms of compensation, there is the potential for abuse if the advisor starts working with you on a fee basis and, after gaining your trust, a year later starts presenting high commission based annuity products. Of course, a good Fee-based advisor wouldn't do this, but the potential temptations exist. A good Fee-based advisor may offset his fees with the commissions that he makes from the sale of any commissioned based products and he should make this clear to you at the outset.

Fee-Only Advisor

I believe that working with a Fee-Only advisor gives you the best chance of working with a truly trustworthy financial advisor because you are aware of the form of compensation from the outset and it presents the fewest opportunities for conflicts of interest. There are several forms of Fee-Only planners: you can pay for services by the hour; you can pay a flat project fee or annual retainer; or you can pay an annual fee based on a percentage of assets that are managed. Some Fee-Only advisors may offer you a choice in how they work; more experienced advisors may not.

The truly Fee-Only compensated advisor cannot sell you commissioned products so, if he recommends that you need long-term care insurance, you can shop around and buy it from anyone. The advisor is in a better position to give you truly objective financial advice.

You do need to be sure that you are working with a truly Fee-Only advisor since many Fee-based advisors will tell you they work Fee-Only. Since the Fee-Only advisor is being paid only by you, he is motivated to find you investment products with no commissions and low expenses.

For people of modest means or uncomplicated financial planning needs an hourly- only advisor may be best, but I think most of the benefit people get is from having an open, ongoing relationship with an advisor. If the billing clock is ticking every time you call the advisor most people won't call as often as they should. If your financial situation is more complicated due to having more assets, I think you would be better off with a Fee-Only advisor who works on an annual retainer or a percentage of the assets under management.

As I said earlier, no form of compensation is without the potential for abuse, although I believe Fee-Only has the least. The difficulty that you will most likely have is finding one, since there is a shortage of experienced Fee-Only advisors who act as both financial planners and investment advisors. Most who have been in business a while will require a fairly high minimum annual fee to work with them.

They require a large minimum because they may only be making a 1% a year fee. The nature of the Fee-Only advisor's work is very labor-intensive and he must keep you satisfied every year since you are not locked into a long-term contract. If you have over $500,000 to be managed, this type of advisor would make the most sense for you.

NAPFA

I believe The National Association of Personal Financial Advisors (NAPFA), to me, represents the elite of the personal financial advisors in this country. There are only about 1000 members nationwide and the qualifying criteria to being a NAPFA member are fairly tough.

NAPFA members must be truly Fee-Only, accept no commissions whatsoever, and never accept any referral or kickback fees. In addition, members must submit to an initial background investigation and ongoing verification of a clean regulatory record. Most importantly applicants must prove they can offer comprehensive financial planning in addition to just investment advice by being required to submit a full financial plan for peer review by existing NAPFA members. If the plan isn't good enough, the application is denied. Now you understand why there are only about 1000 members nationwide.

If you are looking for a new personal financial advisor, I suggest you start your search by contacting NAPFA (800-366-2732) or going to their website **www.napfa.org**. NAPFA will provide you with a list of names of members in your area. Also, you should request their free and excellent *How To Select A Financial Advisor* form and their *Comprehensive Financial Planning Checklist*, which will give you good questions to ask when interviewing a potential new financial advisor.

Credentials & Designations

There are several different credentials and designations that you can look for when trying to find a trusted advisor. There are also many that are totally meaningless, except they enable someone to be impressed by putting a lot of letters behind one's name on a business card.

Of course a credential or designation is just a starting point. Experience and wisdom, especially when working with investments, is more important than any designation because the stock market is the ultimate school of hard knocks. It can provide one with a very good education but at a very expensive tuition rate. You are better off working with someone who has already paid the price the market extracts from the inexperienced advisor's clients.

I have met some very bright financial advisors who have multiple degrees and more designations than can fit on a business card but they lack basic common sense or they have the personality of a stone. You need to find someone whose personality you can work with and feel comfortable with.

A good personal financial advisor is someone who is basically frugal (if he wastes all of his money, what will happen to yours?); has to have good technical investment skills; and must have good communication skills so you can understand what he is saying. Most importantly, when it comes to investing, he must have a disciplined, skeptical personality and a little bit of street smarts. Making money in the stock market is part science and part art.

The CERTIFIED FINANCIAL PLANNER™ Practitioner, (CFP®)

The CERTIFIED FINANCIAL PLANNER™ practitioner is currently the gold standard for selecting a personal financial advisor. This title signifies a well-rounded education in the area of personal finance. The CFP® program requires the completion of at least five courses covering financial planning, taxes, insurance, investments, estate planning and sometimes others.

The certification is awarded and enforced by the CERTIFIED FINANCIAL PLANNER™ Board of Standards. In order for someone to become a CERTIFIED FINANCIAL PLANNER™ professional, she takes a course of study at a college or university in a financial planning program, must pass a rigorous 10-hour exam and have at least 3 years experience in the field of financial planning. In addition, there are continuing education requirements and an approved course in ethics that must be taken every 2 years. To check on a CERTIFIED FINANCIAL PLANNER™ professional's history, go to www.cfp-board.org, click on "Consumers" button, and scroll down to find "Check up on a financial planner." There are several options; click on "Verify your planners CFP® certification".

Personal Financial Specialists (CPA/PFS)

This is a CPA who has met other criteria in order to obtain the PFS designation, Personal Financial Specialist. The CPA must pass a comprehensive six-hour exam covering six financial planning topics. The CPA must also have 120 hours every 3 years of continuing education with 72 hours of financial planning courses, with each hour documented in prescribed disciplines and subject to audit. This designation is held by a CPA who wants to expand his practice to incorporate financial planning and investment advice.

Chartered Financial Consultant (ChFC)

ChFC is a financial planning designation for the insurance industry awarded by the American College. ChFCs must meet experience requirements and pass exams covering finance and investing. They must have at least three years of experience in the financial industry, and have studied and passed an examination on the fundamentals of financial planning, including income tax, insurance, investment and estate planning.

Chartered Financial Analyst (CFA)

CFA is a professional designation given by the CFA Institute (formerly AIMR) that measures the competence and integrity of financial analysts. Candidates are required to pass three levels of exams covering areas such as accounting, economics, ethics, money management, and security analysis. This designation is mostly for Wall Street analysts and institutional money managers. The person with this designation would usually work as an analyst researching investments with not much training in personal finance.

Registered Investment Advisor (RIA)

A major part of how a good advisor helps ensure that you have a successful retirement plan is by helping you manage your investments. In order to do that, the advisor must be registered with the proper authorities. If the advisor is managing less than $25 million then he is registered and monitored by his particular state. Surprisingly, most states do very little monitoring of their advisors and there are very few criteria to becoming registered. You complete the paperwork and pay the annual fees, with each state enforcing their registered advisors differently.

When an advisor is managing over $25 million he will register with the Securities and Exchange Commission (SEC). The SEC is the financial watchdog for all federally-registered investment advisors and they have very strict rules that must be followed. The SEC does random audits of federally registered investment advisors and it is not uncommon for them to stay in an advisor's office for as long as a week looking over trading practices, emails, performance claims and just about anything they want to examine.

In the past few years, since all of the insider and mutual fund trading scandals were uncovered, the SEC has gotten even tougher in their requirements. It has become an expensive and a time-consuming burden for smaller independent advisors to meet all of the compliance requirements from the SEC.

In your advisor selection process you should try to work with a firm that is federally registered with the SEC. You can be sure that the compliance criteria are tougher and that the auditing staff is much larger. Also, the fact that someone is managing over $25 million gives you a little idea of how successful his investment strategies have been. If someone has been in business over 10 years and manages less than $25 million, I would want to know why. Is it because he lost all of his clients' money during the DOT COM days, or perhaps he just wants to stay very small? In any case, I would want to understand why.

RIAs registered with the SEC have to keep undated files called ADV part 1 and part 2 with the SEC that describe how they practice, how they get paid and if there have been any complaints against them. You should receive a copy of the advisor's ADV part 2 prior to working with him and you can review any financial advisor's ADV part 1 online by going on the Internet to <u>www.adviserinfo.sec.gov</u>. Go to the investment adviser search section and put the name of the firm in.

Difference Between an RIA and a Broker

In a nutshell the main difference is the broker is a sales agent for his firm and has a primary responsibility to his firm, while an RIA has a fiduciary requirement to put his client's interest first when making any decision. Most people fail to understand this difference and currently the Financial Planning Association is suing the SEC to try to get brokers who hold themselves out as financial advisors to conform to the same fiduciary requirements that registered investment advisors are required to.

The large brokerage firms have very deep pockets and spend millions of dollars in advertising to get you to believe that they have your best interest at heart. If you do a Google search of SEC fines and penalties paid by most of the large brokerage firms, you will find it not uncommon to see fines of over $100 million for abusive illegal activity that harmed their clients.

Independent Advisors

An independent financial advisor is someone who doesn't work for a firm but operates his own enterprise. While he will have an affiliation with a custodian or a broker dealer (which is needed in order to buy and sell your investments), the advisor is free to switch firms if he is not satisfied with their service.

When you work with an independent advisor you are usually working directly with the owner of the firm (if it is a small firm) or the owner is actively involved with what is going on each day. In order to remain in business, the independent advisor has to give you good service.

The independent advisor is free to offer the services he believes are best for his clients. If he wants to specialize in upper middle-class retirees without children, he is free to do that. If he wants to work with mostly medical doctors, that's how he will gear his practice.

Since no one is telling the advisor what to do or how to do it, this allows the advisor the flexibility to give more objective advice to his clients even if it results in less short-term profitability for his firm.

Just because an advisor is independent doesn't mean he is ethical or honest. You still have to make that determination. What it does mean is that no one is breathing down his neck, forcing him to take some unsound action like pushing some inappropriate products on his clients just to make the corporation's quarterly profit number.

Financial Planning Takes Time and Experience

In the chapter on retirement planning I mentioned that it is money well spent to have an objective professional do your retirement planning with you. I say *with you* because you still have to play a major role in the process. An offsetting benefit is that, in most cases, the planner's fee is tax-deductible. While getting a tax deduction is great, locating someone to work with may be challenging.

Finding an objective CERTIFIED FINANCIAL PLANNER™ professional to help you with your retirement decisions is not as easy as you might think. The reason it is so difficult to find a competent objective financial planner is that good, objective financial planning requires a lot of time and most clients don't want to pay for the expertise. It is easier for the planner to make money working with investments and not planning.

Part of the problem is that the large brokerage houses and conglomerate financial firms are using financial plans as a loss leader in order to sell more expensive, more profitable financial products. They produce very good-looking reports in a nice binder for under $500 and you believe that this is a good plan.

What you don't realize is they lost money (if they did it correctly) doing your plan. In most cases, the representative you are working with is only having you complete a questionnaire and sending the data off to someone else to complete.

The problem is that in order to do more detailed planning (people with $500,000 + assets usually have more complicated financial situations). You need to have a very sophisticated financial-planning, cash-flow driven, software-modeling tool.

The better financial-planning software requires a much higher level of skill to use properly and a longer learning curve for the financial planner to be competent with the software.

Work With An Advisor/Planner

When selecting a financial advisor you should try to work with someone who will not only manage your investments but will also do your retirement planning. The advisor may have most of the work done with an in-house certified Para- planner, but he should be involved with the entire process and have the meetings with you. Here's why.

As I said in the opening of the last chapter, to a RINK, a good longstanding relationship with a trusted advisor should be a cornerstone of your successful retirement strategy and the advisor should be the quarterback of your $Team. When a financial advisor works through the financial planning process with you, he gets a much better understanding of you, your needs, wants and desires.

The conversations that you have during the planning process help the advisor to better know you and this affects his interactions with you and the advice he gives you throughout your long professional relationship together. It is not the same thing if the advisor is getting the information second hand or just off of a data-gathering form. The planning process helps you develop trust in your new advisor and this is very important.

Many financial advisors I know just want to concentrate on managing a client's investments. While this is very important for a RINK you need much more support with other financial issues. Doing planning for clients is very time- consuming, requires a wider breadth of skills to stay current on issues, and is less profitable. In fact, many times the advisor who does the planning will charge the same annual fee as the advisor who just manages your investments! Give yourself a better resource for help by working with an advisor who also does real financial and retirement planning.

Your Search For The Trusted Advisor/Planner

You should start your search by looking for a Fee-Only, independent financial advisor who can also provide you with comprehensive financial planning. But how do you go about finding someone? The best place to start is by contacting NAPFA, as I mentioned before, and asking for a list of their members in your area, but you would still have to narrow down that list and you may not find someone you like. You could also contact your local Financial Planners Association (FPA) Chapter and ask for names of people in your area that fit the criteria that you are seeking. In addition the FPA has a website to help locate financial planners, www.fpanet.org

Many people ask friends and relatives for referrals. That can be both good and bad. The friends and relatives you are asking may have completely different needs than you. They may have brokers who only buy them muni bonds and they are happy with them. Since you are looking for a more comprehensive advisor, you will need to ask more detailed questions.

Just because of the nature of this business, it sometimes seems that the more successful, sales- oriented financial people tend to have very dynamic personalities. They are outgoing, fun and good conversationalists, whereas many of the really good financial advisors I know have a more analytical, less-outgoing personality. The point that I'm trying to make here is that if your friend says his broker or advisor is a "great guy" make sure you understand what that means. You are looking for someone who will help you make sound, honest, financial decisions all during retirement, not someone who is a good cheerleader whom you would enjoy having at your birthday party.

Read, Understand and Then Call

In your search for an advisor try to read as much about each firm as possible before you contact them. Most financial advisors have a website that acts as an electronic brochure. You can take a look at mine to get an idea of what to expect at www.raymignone. com

Read as much as you can about the advisor. The more information provided on the website, the more comfortable you should feel. The website should discuss the advisor's services, if he does financial planning, or if he provides investment management services. The website should contain a short biography about the advisor with a photograph to help you get to know him better. There should also be information explaining the advisor's philosophy on overall planning and investments. If you are looking for someone to build a strategic, long-term, diversified portfolio, you don't want to hire a firm that highlights aggressive trading, for example.

The website should also contain information on articles the advisor has been featured in or has written himself, and what professional organizations and board positions he has held in the past. The website might also list the advisor's fees and if he has a minimum requirement of assets in order for new clients to work with him.

The fantastic thing about an advisor's website is you can get a really good understanding of the way the advisor works without having to even contact his firm. I think most people find this a less objectionable way to learn about someone rather than to be put in an awkward situation. Also, don't forget to look up the advisor on the SEC website for past violations and to see if he gets paid by commissions or not.

Call The Advisor

At this point, you have good background information on the advisor, you have eliminated the advisors whose information you didn't like, and so you should make a call to set up a *get to know you* appointment. Advisory firms will handle this next step differently, depending on how much new business they want (or need!). Most advisors will offer a complimentary first meeting either on the phone or in person.

At this meeting please don't expect to get free advice but, rather, to hear, in person, the services offered; you both get to basically interview each other. Before I set up an appointment with a new prospective client, I like to talk to her on the phone for 15 or 20 minutes to get a chance to understand her needs and to also make sure my services are appropriate for her.

What is the point of wasting your time dragging yourself in for an appointment if you can find out on the phone in 15 minutes that the advisor can't help you with something you need, such as international tax law? I think you should talk on the phone first, even if the advisor doesn't insist on it.

The First Meeting

Let's say your phone conversation went well, you and the advisor think there is a good fit, and you set up an initial meeting. As I said before, unless you are told otherwise, this should be a complimentary meeting. If you are not sure, ask first. These first meetings usually last about one hour and, if you are married, you should bring your spouse. Part of the reason to develop a long-term relationship with your advisor is so that there is someone you can trust that will not take advantage of your surviving spouse should something happen to you.

To make the initial meeting more productive you need to give the advisor an idea of your total net worth, income and what you're trying to accomplish. The advisor will tell you what you should bring to the meeting. Since your goal is to ensure a comfortable lifestyle during retirement, with dignity and independence, also let the advisor know you don't have children to assist you when you get older.

Questions To Ask At The First Meeting

You should bring a list of questions to ask the advisor. Have them written down before you come in so you don't forget. You are trying to determine if the advisor can meet your needs, that is, help you with retirement projections, manage your portfolio during retirement and if he is familiar with planning strategies for someone with your wealth who has no children.

Some Questions You Should Ask

✶ Who will work with me, you or an associate?

✶ How long have you been in practice?

✶ Do you have other clients like me?

✶ Can you still work with me if I move away?

I would like to discuss some of these questions because I believe it is important for you to understand that when you are interviewing a financial advisor, your decision to hire that person is extremely critical to you, since this is the person you expect to be the leader of your $Team. You should also realize that some advisors are so hungry for new clients they may initially pretend to do whatever it takes to get your business, so the more you ask, the better. Ask:

Who will work with me? You want to know ahead of time who will be your financial advisor, the person whose name is on the door whom you did all the research on, or an associate? Preferably, you will want to work with the main advisor; sure the staff will handle your administrative issues, but when you have financial planning or investment questions, you want to work with an experienced advisor.

Some firms as they grow have a team approach; there is a main advisor and other team advisors assigned to your team. This may work out fine if the team is experienced, but I think it is important to know this ahead of time to decide if that will be acceptable to you.

How long have you been in practice? It's important to find out how much experience someone has as a financial advisor. The more experience the more different situations he has experienced. While I don't think you need someone with 20 years of experience, someone with at least 10 years' experience, especially if he had other previous, related experience, should be fine. If you were just starting out and you were 30 years old with just a $50,000 portfolio, a less- experienced advisor would be fine, but this is not acceptable for you; there is too much at stake.

Do you have other clients like me? While most financial advisors will have some variety of clients, the better advisors, once established will tend to focus on a few main types of clients with similar asset levels. You are looking for an advisor who works with retirees who have significant net wealth.

If most of the advisor's clients have $1million or more, you can be sure he has been involved with more sophisticated tax, estate and charitable planning strategies. This would be more appropriate for someone like you without children. He will also have a network of other experienced professionals that he has worked with in the past. One clue to finding his average client's net worth is to ask what is the minimum asset requirement to work with him. If he only requires you to have $200,000 and you have $2,000,000, you are most likely not like his average client.

What is your investment philosophy? You need to completely understand the advisor's investment philosophy to make sure it is compatible with your personality. If the advisor tells you that he aims to beat the stock market in performance each year, that may not fit in with your goal of steady risk controlled growth.

Shopping for an advisor just based on past investment performance will get you in trouble. First of all, most advisors don't have audited performance returns, so how do you know what they really did over the past few years? They could tell you just about anything. Find an advisor who has a well-balanced, long-term approach to investing and you will most likely do fine. Stay away from the gunslinger, since you may get shot!

Can you still work with me if I move away? Today, with the Internet and current communication technology, many financial advisors are able to keep working with you even when you move to the other side of the country. In many cases, people retire and want to move to a warmer or less expensive area but still maintain the advisor/client relationship.

I have many clients who have moved out of state and so we never meet face to face again. I also have a few clients who live far away who came from referrals. I have never met these clients in person. Using the phone, fax, mail, email, client conference calls and web meetings, your advisor can maintain very good communications with you even if you are far away.

We use a software product that allows us to easily hold a web meeting with the client so she can see all of her reports instantly on her own computer screen while we talk on the phone. Everything I do on my computer screen is reflected on hers. The technology works great, it's easy to use and it's almost like being in the office having a review meeting in person. The only complaint we get from clients is that they miss the warm cup of Cappuccino that they get when in our office. If you find a trusted advisor and you decide to move, you should still be able to maintain a good working relationship.

Advisor/Client Relationship

Now you have found and retained your advisor and decided to have him do your planning and manage your investments. You can expect a good advisor to explain the process of what you will need to do next, handle all of your account transfers and set up the meetings to discuss your investment policy and your financial planning.

Don't be afraid to ask questions if you don't understand something, but please let the advisor do his job. You hired the advisor, and you are paying him good money, so allow him to help you by listening to what he recommends and following up on any action items that come out of your planning meeting. Many times you are not comfortable initially with all of the changes that are being made and that is normal. You have been handling your money a certain way all of your life, so change is a little scary.

The experienced advisor should know the best way to manage your money, based on his years of experience and your agreed- to Investment Policy Statement.

Try to concentrate on the bottom line and not the details. For example, when reviewing your investments, concentrate on the overall investment return and not the performance of each individual investment. The advisor may have placed that particular investment in your portfolio because he knows how it fits in with all of your other investments and it is only one building block. Most good advisors concentrate on the overall portfolio's risk/reward characteristics and not the individual investments.

If you call your advisor every month and want to discuss why XYZ Fund underperformed all other funds in the same Morningstar category you will frustrate both the advisor and yourself and the relationship won't last. The example I like to give clients is that your portfolio is like the transmission in your car. It has many moving gears inside. Some are turning forward, some are turning backward at the same time, but what you should care about is that your car is reliable, safe and goes forward when you put it into drive. If your car doesn't go forward when it's supposed to, that's what you need to talk about, not each individual gear.

An Advisor Can Be Helpful In Other Ways

You should expect your advisor to be available to speak with you on a broad array of issues. Most people incorrectly think that a financial advisor can only help you with making money. You will find, as your relationship with the advisor matures, he could help you with many other issues, perhaps not even directly dealing with money.

This is why I believe that, especially for RINKs, it is important to have a good, long- established relationship with your advisor as you mature into retirement and why I recommend an advisor who is not just a money manager, since the money manager won't be answering lifestyle questions from other clients that may also be helpful to you. The advisor who has many other clients in similar situations to you will be experienced with issues such as, which is the best local medical plan, how will buying a second home in Florida affect my local income taxes, how much should I expect to pay to get my kitchen remodeled, and numerous other issues.

The advisor will have local contacts with good insurance people, real estate agents and may even have experience with nursing homes in your area. If he doesn't know something you asked he probably could recommend someone who can help you, so don't be afraid to ask such questions of the advisor or his staff, even if you think it has nothing to do with your professional relationship. A good advisor and his team want to help and will go out of their way whenever possible. Don't be afraid to call your advisor's office with your non-money questions.

Is Hiring The Advisor Worth The Money?

Of course this is something you have to decide for yourself, but all I can say is that the people who have found a good, trusted advisor are usually financially better off and worry less about their financial situation. There are some people who feel comfortable and capable to handle all of the issues I discussed in this book themselves, so they may not need an advisor. Sometimes investing in the stock market is a big part of someone's life, sort of his hobby and he won't give that up. In that case an advisor is probably not for him.

Based on my experience, most people don't have the time, inclination or the right emotional temperament to do a good job handling their own finances and investments. They tend to get sidetracked too easily from their original plans, don't follow up on strategies, and end up making bad investment changes at the wrong time.

While there may be some unethical people in the financial advisory business, I think they are the minority. There are also some very excellent financial advisors who, for all the reasons I mentioned in this book, will earn their fees many times over, providing valuable services for their clients. The challenge is for you to find a good, trusted advisor and that's why I have included so much material discussing this topic. If you find that good advisor, you won't need to know all the other things in this book; he will.

Expect To Pay For An Experienced Advisor

An experienced, ethical financial advisor is well paid for his work. If you understand how you will benefit from his services, it should prove to be an excellent value for you. A Fee-Only advisor only gets paid from you and he is not compensated by anyone else so, when you see the fee deducted from your account, it appears to be a lot of money and, in some cases, it is. But you have to ask yourself: do you want to work with someone who is successful, ethical and experienced, or someone inexperienced and unproven?

Someone selling you an annuity insurance product can earn possibly 10% or more selling that one transaction and never has to service you as a client again. It would take 10 years for a good Fee-Only advisor to make the same amount of money working with you. Think about that!

Chapter Summary

In this chapter I suggest that it isn't easy finding a good trusted financial advisor and so you should start your search early. Since the advisor should be the lead person on your $Team, you need to be sure you have the right person before you enter the later stages of your retirement.

Since anyone can call himself a financial advisor, it will take a little work on your part to find a good one. One way to evaluate different advisors is to find out how they are paid: Commissions, Fee-based or Fee-Only. While no form of compensation is without potential abuse, the Fee-Only model seems to have the least amount of conflicts since you pay the advisor directly.

A good starting point to finding a Fee-Only advisor would be to contact NAPFA (800-366-2732) or go to their website www.napfa.org. Be sure to also request some of their consumer materials on how to interview an advisor.

You will find many designations when evaluating advisors. While these are important, I believe experience and personality may be more important to a successful relationship.

Independent RIAs have a fiduciary responsibility to put their client's interests first. Stockbrokers working for a large firm do not have the same responsibility, since they are sales agents for their firm.

It is hard to find someone who will just do financial planning for you, since the planner has difficulty making money just doing true planning. Most of the large firms just concentrate on investments, since that is the most profitable area of the business.

When you get referrals from your friends for an advisor, be sure the advisor has the services that you need, which may be different from your friends' needs.

It is a good idea to spend time reviewing an advisor's website and speaking on the phone with the advisor prior to setting up the first meeting to ensure he is a good fit for you.

Be prepared to ask questions at the initial interview meeting such as; How do you get paid? Who will work with me?

When starting to work with the advisor, allow him to implement his strategy and try to concentrate on the big picture, not the individual details. Don't be afraid to ask your advisor questions not directly related to your money. He will try to help if possible.

Hiring a financial advisor is not for everyone. If you do find a good, experienced, trusted advisor, you will have to pay well for his services, but, in return, you should receive very good value for your money.

10) Charitable Giving

I have found that among its other benefits,
giving liberates the soul of the giver.

-Maya Angelou

As a financially successful RINK, you are in the unique position of being able to give away some of your money while you are alive and pass on your assets to help causes that are important to you once you are gone. Leaving a large estate to children or grandchildren is not an option for you. Yes, you may want to leave some money to relatives and friends, but more and more RINKs are getting involved with charitable giving. Charitable giving is a deeply personal expression of your beliefs and life experience.

In this chapter I want to address some of the strategies for controlled gifting while you are alive, as well as making charitable gifting part of your overall estate plan. You will see that there are some very smart ways that you can give to charities and get the maximum tax benefit from the gift. This means you are making part of the donation and Uncle Sam is making the other part of the donation, but you control which charity receives the benefit. As enticing as the tax benefits are, these contributions do not offset the loss of wealth to you and your all-important requirement to maintain a large retirement nest egg.

Your charitable giving must come from your sincere desire to support and provide for one or more charities with a true gift of your heart. If you don't have a sincere charitable intent, then the best of these strategies are not for you since, in all of them, you end up permanently giving away some of your money. Once again, you must fall back to your retirement projections and your current financial position to be sure you can afford the gifting while you are alive.

Personally Getting Involved Volunteering

While the other strategies I will discuss involve giving away your money, volunteering will allow you to give away part of your life. If you find a cause that you are passionate about, donating your time will give you great emotional reward. You will also be in a better position to determine whether the charity deserves your money. What better way to see where your donations will go? In addition, getting involved with a charity that you are passionate about will help you make friends that can become part of your all-important Emotional ETeam. Working together doing charitable work all during the year keeps you in close contact with individuals who already have a compassionate heart and will be more predisposed to help you in your time of need.

To make volunteering successful, you should find a cause you are passionate about and then go to work doing what you like doing using your life experiences. The experience you gained in achieving your own freedom as a RINK can be the gift you give to the charitable organization you choose. If you were in sales/marketing, then why not help with fundraising and promotion of the charity? If you were an attorney, why not help the charity with their various legal issues? What the charity needs most of all is your experience. If you decide to just stuff envelopes once a month I think you will get pretty bored. There are so many different charitable organizations I'm sure you can find one that would be a good fit for you.

Outright Donations

Of course, you can always just write a check to your favorite charity and take the tax deduction on your income tax return. Once you write a check for over $250, you must receive a written acknowledgement from the charity and the charity needs to be a charity recognized by the IRS. An organization that says, "We are tax exempt" does not necessarily mean that contributions are tax deductible. *Tax exempt* simply means the organization does not have to pay taxes. *Tax deductible* means the donor can deduct contributions to the organization on his or her federal income tax return. The Internal Revenue Code defines more than 20 different categories of tax-exempt organizations, but contributions to only a few of these categories are also tax deductible. Principal among tax-deductible groups is the 501(c)(3) category, broadly termed charitable organizations. In general, you need to find out if the charity is a legitimate 501 (c)(3) charity.

To obtain tax exempt status under Section 501(c)(3), an organization has to file documents with the Internal Revenue Service that prove it to be organized and operated for the charitable purposes specified by the Internal Revenue Code. The IRS looks at these documents only in terms of the code; it does not "approve" specific charities or judge other aspects of the charity's efficiency. Organizations receiving 501(c)(3) status are those that the IRS has considered charitable, educational, religious, scientific, or literary; those that prevent cruelty to animals: and those that foster national or international amateur sports competitions.

The simplicity of making a direct cash donation is what makes it so appealing. You control how much is given, to whom and when you make the gift, thus controlling the year in which you get the tax deduction. Normally, if you make a cash donation or a donation of unappreciated property, you can take a deduction for charitable contributions that cannot exceed 50% of your adjusted gross income (AGI) for the year you make the donation. A reduced donation applies to appreciated assets. Contributions that exceed the AGI limit in the current year can be carried over to each of the five succeeding years. Carryover contributions are subject to the original percentage limits in the carryover years.

Donate Appreciated Property

Gifting *appreciated property* usually is the best way to leverage your donations. As part of our service we like to review our client's income tax return, especially new clients, and when I see large charitable contributions we have the discussion whether there is a better way to make donations. The better way is to give the charity appreciated assets that you might have, especially very low basis individual stock positions you have owned for a long time that have large gains. The benefits of gifting the appreciated asset are twofold. You get a larger tax benefit and you eliminate or reduce a consolidated position that perhaps was too large a percentage of your entire portfolio.

Many new clients come to me holding mutual funds and single stock positions that they have had for so many years that their gain if sold would be 200% or more of the original position and in many cases they have no idea what they paid for it. Rather than having the nightmare of trying to determine what they paid, they just keep the position. These assets are prime candidates for gifting away.

Let me try to give you an example: say you want to donate money to your favorite charity for a new project they are working on and you own $22,000 worth of IBM stock that you bought years ago with a cost of only $2,000. If you sold the stock, you would have to pay long-term capital gains on the $20,000 gain. Currently, the federal long-term capital gains rate is low, at a maximum rate of 15%, but then you have your state income tax to pay, so your total tax rate on the gain could be 22%. That would be $4,400 in taxes on the $20,000 gain, leaving you with $17,600 from your sale of $22,000 of IBM stock. If you wanted you could then write the check to your charity for $17,600 and get a tax deduction for the $17,600 donation.

A better way would be to arrange for your custodian to have the shares of IBM stock wired directly to the charity at the current value of $22,000 (Many charities are set up to accept these transfers). This way you do not pay any capital gains tax and the charity sells it immediately and pockets the entire $22,000, since the charity doesn't pay taxes. The benefits to you are: you reduced an unwanted investment position, you didn't have to research the cost of the IBM stock, you didn't have to pay any capital gains on the sale, and you get to deduct the full $22,000 as a charitable contribution instead of only $17,600. You may only be limited to deduct up to 20% or 30% of your AGI in any one year. When you donate appreciated assets, the determination of exactly how much can be deducted in one year can get a little complicated to explain here, so be sure to discuss this with your tax advisor. In any case, if you can't deduct it all in the year of donating because your AGI is too low, the balance can be carried forward for up to 5 years. Whenever possible, gift appreciated assets.

Strategies To Donate Appreciated Assets

You should think about the timing of when to donate appreciated assets in order to maximize the tax benefit. There are years when your income may be exceptionally high: perhaps you were given a large bonus, cashed in stock options, sold your business or sold a rental property that had a large gain. Such years when you have unusually large income would be the years to donate the appreciated assets.

Since you will be in the highest tax bracket in these special years, you will get the most benefit from the donation. If you don't want the charity to get all of the money in the high earning year but you still want the deduction, there are ways to accomplish this also, which I will discuss shortly. Keep in mind you can donate any appreciated asset, including real estate, as long as the charity will accept it.

If you are thinking of making a donation and you own a mutual fund with a large gain that, in addition, you expect will pay out a large, year-end short-term taxable gain distribution, you should gift the mutual fund *before* it makes the distribution. That way you avoid the capital gain tax, the short- term gain tax (mutual fund short-term capital gains distributions are taxed as regular income), and you get the tax deduction for the full amount of the current value. A triple win!

Deduct Now, Donate Later

There are ways that you can make a gift of an appreciated asset in the year you need the deduction while actually sending checks to the charities over several years. This makes sense when you need to increase your deductions, so you wish to make a very large gift, but the gift is larger than what you feel comfortable giving away in one year.

For example, you normally give charitable donations of $10,000 a year. In the year 2006, you took a large buyout retirement package from your employer because the offer was too good to refuse. You also had to cash in stock options and, since you decided to move from N.Y.C. to Florida, you sold your rental property in N.Y. Normally your AGI ran about $150,000 a year, but this year your taxable AGI will be close to $1 million, pushing you into the very top federal tax bracket. In addition, you live in N.Y.C. so, on top of the current federal 35% tax bracket, you will pay approximately another 11% in N.Y. state and city income taxes.

In the next year 2007 you will be retired, living in Florida, a tax friendly state which has no state income tax, and you expect to only be in the 15% federal tax bracket. While you want to continue your normal $10,000 a year charitable donations in retirement, you won't receive much value from the tax deduction in future years since you will be in the lower tax bracket.

The following are vehicles that will solve your problem. I'll start with the one most people should use because of its simplicity. That is donor-advised funds. Next, I will cover more complicated strategies.

Donor Advised Funds

Donor advised funds have grown immensely popular in recent years. They provide the immediate tax benefits of an irrevocable gift while also allowing you time to decide which public charities you would like to receive *grants*. A variety of charitable organizations, community foundations, mutual funds and custodians like Vanguard, Fidelity and Charles Schwab offer donor-advised funds.

Donor-advised funds accept donations of cash or appreciated securities. After you contribute, the organization establishes an account and invests your gift in pools of specified investments, usually mutual funds. Once the account is opened you assume the role of account advisor. You receive periodic statements reporting the account's current market value, any new contributions to the account and any grants paid from your account. The *grants* are what they call the checks when mailed to the charity.

You will appoint yourself the *account advisor* and you can make a *successor advisor*. Once you make the donation, you will no longer own the assets from the gift but you can change the investment options as well as suggest the gifts to be made. The charity that you recommend to receive the grant must be a *qualified charity* and the donor-advised fund would help verify that for you. Once the fund approves your charity, they send a check to the charity noting your name (unless you request to remain anonymous).

You receive accounts statements showing the performance of your remaining investments and the history of the grants. Most donor-advised funds have Internet access, so you can track your account online. You can also make arrangements for someone to continue to be the account advisor when you die or you can specify the charity or charities of your choice that the balance of the account will be paid out to, when you pass on.

A donor-advised fund is the best way for most people to take advantage of the "deduct now, donate later" strategy. The donor-advised funds offered by the custodians allow you to take the deduction now, and give you flexibility in the timing of the charitable donations, and enable you to see your gifts grow in value over time inside your account. The fund handles all of the regulatory paperwork, so this makes your life much less complicated.

It is important to understand the minimum required donations needed to start the fund. Some allow you to start with only $5,000; others require $25,000 or more. Also, investigate the investment options available and, most importantly, the fees and expenses that will be charged to you.

The Family Foundation

A family foundation or private foundation works similar to the donor-advised funds, except you have much more control. It is a way to create a perpetual legacy of charitable giving for your descendants while accomplishing significant estate planning objectives. Many of the very wealthiest families establish family foundations.

With the family foundation, you are essentially establishing your own tax-exempt organization for the purpose of benefiting charities. While you have much more control with your funds in a family foundation it is expensive and complicated to set up and maintain.

You will have to have an attorney create the initial documents. In addition, you will have annual tax filing requirements and federal reporting requirements. You can find firms that will handle everything for you since they have boilerplate documents. They will handle all of the tax filings and compliance work, but they will want to control the checkbook. The annual fees usually run around $5,000 a year and up. One such company is Foundationsource in Connecticut (1 800-839-0054 www. foundationsource.com).

Charitable Remainder Trusts (CRT)

Now we are getting to some of the more complicated charitable and estate planning strategies that you could use and I have used with clients. Please keep in mind that these trusts can be expensive to set up and maintain, but are good if you want to have the most control and they only make economic sense if you have a charitable intent.

Yet, with smart planning, these can be a good planning technique to help diversify your existing portfolio with low cost-basis stock. The following are two variations of Charitable Remainder Trusts (CRT).

Charitable Remainder Annuity Trusts (CRAT)

The *Charitable Remainder Annuity Trust* (CRAT) is a way to take appreciated non-income –producing property and convert it into assets that can provide you with current income. With a CRAT, you receive a fixed dollar amount each year. When the trust is created, you specify the payout as a percentage of the fair market value of the assets when placed in the trust.

You have some leeway with the percentage you can use. Keep in mind there is a relationship between the percentage used for withdrawals and the amount you can deduct. This requires complicated tax planning with a knowledgeable advisor to find the right balance. The payout must conform to IRS guidelines and, while you get the payout each year, when you die the charity gets the balance of the proceeds. Let me give an example.

Let's say you are in your 70s and you own a beachfront lot in the Hamptons on Long Island. The property is worth $1 million and you paid $100,000 for it years ago. Since it is vacant land, you don't receive any income from it so you decide that you want to receive some current income but hate to pay the capital gains tax. You work with your advisor and attorney to create a CRAT, the attorney draws up the documents, and you choose a 6% return. Since you are creating your own CRAT (which I recommend, since you have more control over the investments), you make yourself the trustee of the CRAT. The deed gets transferred from your name into the name of the trust and, since you are trustee, you immediately sell the property for $1,000,000 and there is no capital gains tax due since it is a charitable trust.

You will receive an income stream of $60,000 a year (6% on the $1,000,000) for as long as you live or until the money runs out and, when you die, the balance goes to the charity you previously named. If you manage to achieve an annual return on your investments in the trust of over 6% the trust will never run out of money. In addition to the income stream, you receive a $1,000,000 tax deduction on your income tax in the year of donation that you can carry forward for up to 5 years.

As I mentioned earlier, with all charitable donations there are limits of what percentage of your AGI you can deduct in any given year, depending on if you give appreciated assets or cash.

The following example gives you an idea what your income would be if you just sold the property, paid the tax and received 6% on your investment. You see that you would have $48,120 a year income VS the $60,000 a year income from the CRAT.

Sale Of Property:

$1,000,000	Hampton Lot Current Value
-100,000	Cost Basis of Lot
$900,000	Taxable Capital Gain
x 22%	(approx. federal & NY tax)
$198,000	Total Tax On Gain
$1,000,000	Received Upon Sale
-198,000	Total Tax Due
$802,000	Amount You Have To Invest
x 6%	Expected Earnings 6%
$48,120	Annual Income Earned

$60,000 CRAT Income Stream 6%

(AMT is not considered in the above example)

Charitable Remainder Unitrust (CRUT)

A Charitable Remainder Unitrust (CRUT) is similar to the CRAT that we just discussed in that you establish and transfer your assets into the trust, sell the asset and get a tax deduction with an income stream for your life. The balance left when you die goes to the charity that you initially chose. The difference with the CRUT is that the amount you take out each year varies. If we use the same 6% a year withdrawal amount from our previous example, the amount each year was a fixed $60,000. With the CRUT, it would be 6% of the value of the CRUT at a certain date each year, usually the value at the end of the year.

With the CRUT, your annual withdrawal amounts will vary depending on the performance of your portfolio. If the value increases above your initial amount, then you can withdraw more money and, if your value decreases, you will get less money from the CRUT.

One example in which I used a charitable remainder trust was for a RINK client who was widowed, previously named a charity as her primary beneficiary in her will, had very low-cost basis shares of stock that needed to be sold in order to better diversify her portfolio, and had enough other assets to cover any health care needs that would arise during the rest of her life.

I was able to transfer (donate) her low-cost basis stocks into the CRUT, sell her stocks inside the CRUT, buy more diversified mutual funds with the proceeds which we still manage, get a large tax deduction that we have been carrying forward for 3 years now, and now, she gets an annual check from the trust. When she dies the charity inherits whatever is left in the CRUT.

The legal cost to set up a Charitable Remainder Trust is about $5,000 with another $1,000 a year for the tax return preparation. For the right situation, CRTs can be an intelligent way to give to charity.

Exemptions and Maximum Federal Estate Tax Rates

Year	Estate Tax Exemption	Highest Rate
2003	$1 million	49%
2004	$1.5 million	48%
2005	$1.5 million	47%
2006	$2 million	46%
2007	$2 million	45%
2008	$2 million	45%
2009	$3.5 million	45%
2010	N/A (taxes eliminated)	0%
2011	$1 million	60%

Figure 14

Charitable Lead Trusts (CLT) & Pooled Income Funds

Charitable Lead Trusts are best for someone with a *very large amount of assets* that, after a period of time, say 15 to 20 years, will revert back to another person, usually a child. So they aren't the kind of vehicle used by the typical RINK.

Pooled Income Funds can be established with very little money. They are usually set up by the charities themselves and offer some of the benefits of CRTs, that is, tax deduction and liquidation of appreciated assets. When you contribute your money you get a number of interest income units determined by how much you donate. You receive income for a certain period of time or over your lifetime.

Since these funds are usually set up directly with the charity, you have limited flexibility in determining your income or how the money is invested. The money is typically invested in bonds so the income suffers when bonds pay little. Also, the income from the pooled income fund is taxed to you as regular income. You should really understand how a particular pooled income fund works prior to investing your money here.

Charitable Gift Annuities (GCA)

A Charitable Gift Annuity (CGA) is a contract, not a trust, under which a charity, in return for a transfer of cash, marketable securities or other assets, agrees to pay a fixed amount of money to one or two individuals, for their lifetimes.

The person who receives payments is called an annuitant or beneficiary. The fixed payments are fixed and unchanged for the term of the contract. The annuity payments are considered to be a partial tax-free return of the donor's gift, which are spread in equal payments over the life expectancy of the annuitant.

The contributed property you give is irrevocable. It becomes a part of the charity's assets, and the payments are a general obligation of the charity. The annuity is backed by the charity's entire assets, not just by the property contributed. Unlike a trust, annuity payments continue for your life, not only as long as assets remain in the Gift Annuity Fund.

The gift annuity is more tax-friendly than the pooled income funds, since part of the income is considered return of capital. These annuities pay less monthly income than comparable commercially available annuities from life insurance companies.

They only make sense to be considered if you are over 70 years old. Of course, when you die the charity keeps your money and the payments stop. You can shop different charities to see who is willing to pay you more at any given point in time.

Chapter Summary

As a RINK, charitable giving should be a part of your wealth distribution strategy. There are many ways to give, including volunteering, which has the added benefit of involving you with likeminded people who you may form strong bonds with and enlist as part of your ETeam.

When you do make donations you should do so in the most tax advantageous way. This usually means giving low cost-basis appreciated assets instead of just cash.

There are many vehicles available to you to allow different ways to donate, including donor- advised funds which are cost effective and simple, family foundations which make sense for $1,000,000 or more. Different variations of charitable remainder trusts which give you a lot of control, charitable lead trusts which make sense for the very rich only, pooled income funds, and gift annuities which have less flexibility and limited income streams.

While all of these strategies can save on taxes, they don't make economic sense unless you have a charitable intention. If you are like many other RINKs and do intend to pass on some of your wealth to charities, you should look for the smartest strategy possible.

11) Estate Planning

I'm not afraid to die. I just don't want to be there when it happens.
-Woody Allen

When I discuss estate planning with clients, their eyes glaze over because the discussions get complicated, the topic is unappealing, and most people find it boring. The terms used in estate planning are full of legalese and frankly, most people just don't want to think about their own death, especially people who don't have children or grandchildren who will benefit from all of their life's work.

I find it is especially difficult for married couples who don't have children to absorb the idea that their life mate will no longer be with them and they will then be truly alone. While not the most exciting or enjoyable topic, planning for your demise or possible incapacity is very important. You can be like some of my friends who basically say, "I just prefer not to think about it". If that's how you feel then the State will make the decisions for you and you can skip this chapter or you can read on and try and gain a little understanding. While you may not understand completely all of the strategies and estate planning vehicles available to you, I think you should understand enough so that when you work with your advisors you could create a good sound estate and health care plan.

Two Things Are Certain In Life

You know two things are certain in this life: death and taxes. Having a plan that details what happens to your assets when you die is important. When you plan your estate you get to determine how much money your heirs receive and how much goes to Uncle Sam and the State in which you live. For the RINK, estate-planning strategies will differ from individuals who have children since their primary concern may be to leave a large estate to their heirs. For the typical RINK, leaving a large estate to heirs is not the main priority.

You may have relatives or charities that you would like to leave *leftover money* to in the most tax efficient manner possible. How you approach estate planning also is different if you are currently married or if you are on your own. Your goals are to ensure you have enough money while you are living, prepare for illness or incapacitation and, lastly, to leave as much in assets to your chosen beneficiaries while minimizing the amount of expenses and taxes that must be paid.

Of course, your estate planning is more complicated the more assets that you have. I will discuss issues and explain strategies that, as a RINK, you would use to benefit your estate. I will also cover incapacity strategies.

Estate Planning / Elder Law Attorney

When considering any estate planning, you need to work with a qualified estate planning attorney to be sure you are meeting your objectives while making sure your plan conforms to the current laws. Estate planning laws may change several times from the time I write this until you do your planning.

For RINKs I recommend working with an estate-planning attorney that specializes in elder law and elder care planning.

Elder law spans and encompasses elder care planning issues, such as access to the appropriate type of medical and personal care. An elder law attorney can also help with coordinating private and public resources to finance the cost of care, income assistance benefits, taxation, guardianship in addition to general estate planning, estate and trust administration issues (e.g., wills, trusts, and probate).

The elder law attorney may assist with counseling and planning for incapacity with medical directives, advanced directives and other alternative decision-making documents, as well as for possible long-term care planning issues, including home health care, nursing home care, hospice and respite care.

An elder law attorney can help you deal with a multitude of issues, including elder abuse, financial abuse of elders, fraud and other consumer protection issues, nursing home abuse, nursing home impoverishment and nursing home neglect.

You might not think you need these other services now, but why not have your estate planning documents drawn up by someone who has elder law expertise? The elder law attorney may put more emphasis in your estate planning documents on taking care of you, while a regular estate-planning attorney may be more concerned with the taxation of your estate after you are gone. Which is more important to you?

If you want to better understand the services of what an elder law firm could do for you, take a look at the website of Vincent J. Russo & Associates, PC: www.russoelderlaw.com

Basics/Terms/Definitions

An *estate* is all of your assets and all of your liabilities. When you die, your estate becomes a separate legal entity. *Estate planning* is the process of accumulating, protecting and distributing your property in the most effective and efficient manner. A *Will* is your instructions directing how your property will be disposed of upon your demise and it is one of the most basic of estate planning tools.

When you make out your Will you are called a *testator* and when you die you are called a *decedent*; (these are terms you will find in your Will). When you die and have a Will in place, you are said to die *testate;* whereas, if you die without a Will you are said to die *intestate* in which case the state you live in, through its laws will determine how your property is distributed.

A *beneficiary* is someone who receives an inheritance from your estate. *Probate* is the public legal process in which your Will is determined to be valid or not with an *executor* appointed to handle the administration of your estate. This allows for the orderly transfer of ownership of your properties to others. For now, I think this should cover most basic words you will come across in estate planning.

Current Confusing Estate Tax Law

Presently, because of the political compromise in 2001, it is very difficult to know what will happen with the laws regarding the federal estate tax. This makes your planning even more difficult. On May 26, 2001, the U.S. Congress adopted the Economic Growth and Tax Relief Reconciliation Act of 2001. This Act included the largest tax cut in more than 20 years. It also provided for major changes to estate tax, gift tax and the generation-skipping transfer tax (GSTT) starting in the year 2002 and continuing through 2010.

The changes to personal income and estate taxes (including credits, exemptions, etc.) are being phased in starting in 2002 and continue through 2009. In the year 2010, the estate tax and GSTT are repealed for one year. The gift tax, however, continues with a $1 million exemption.

Gifts are currently taxed under the same rates as estates, and the same applicable credit applies to both gifts and estates. Under the Act, the applicable exclusion amount for gift tax purposes is $1 million in 2002 and will remain at that amount until 2009. The applicable exclusion amount for estate tax purposes is currently $2 million in 2006 and increases to $3.5 million in 2009. This means in 2006 you can leave anyone up to $2 million and there is no federal estate tax. Your state may charge an estate tax at a lower level, for example, New York State starts charging estate tax on estates above $1 million.

The biggest change is a new carryover basis system that replaces the estate tax. Under current law, your assets are taxed based on the amount that you own at your death (estate tax). But, your assets also receive a step-up in basis equal to the fair market value of the asset at the time of your death.

Under the new law, during years that the estate tax is repealed, assets do not automatically receive a step-up in basis at your death. The effect of this is an increase in capital gains tax. However, there are provisions for a limited amount of assets to receive a step-up in basis. Up to $3 million of assets transferred to a spouse and $1.3 million of assets transferred to others are eligible for the increased basis at your death. Under this option, the new carryover basis system is applicable for only the one year that the estate tax is repealed. Did I mention this was confusing and makes it difficult to plan? What were the politicians thinking?

There is also something called the *sunset clause*. Because of the sunset clause, the provisions in the Act are effective only to the end of 2010 (in 2010 there is no estate tax!). In 2011 the tax laws revert back to those in place in 2001 unless further legislation is passed. This is the mess that financial planners and estate tax attorneys have to work with when giving you recommendations and drawing up your legal documents. I have included a chart, (Figure 14), which shows the current exemptions and maximum federal estate tax rates.

What I didn't mention is that, between husband and wife, who are US citizens you can transfer an unlimited amount of property and there isn't any estate tax. This has not changed and will not change.

Getting Started

Getting started doing estate planning is probably the hardest part. One of the first things you need to do when you start doing estate planning is to draw up a net worth statement. If you did the retirement planning, as I described in the previous chapter on retirement planning then you should already have created a net worth statement from the software. The Net Worth Statement, (Figure 15), is an example of what we give clients to bring to their estate planning attorney.

Net Worth as of July 2006

	Dick	Jane	Joint	Total
Non-Qualified Assets				
CDs Dick	50,668			50,668
CDs Jane		40,535		40,535
EE Bonds			61,500	61,500
TDW Dick Indiv.	1,287,019			1,287,019
TDW Kristi Jt.		110,011		110,011
TDW Joint			553,001	553,001
TDW Melinda Jt.		110,011		110,011
TDW Jane Ind.		1,207,540		1,207,540
Total Non-Qualified Assets	1,337,687	1,468,097	614,501	3,420,285
Qualified Assets				
TDW Dick IRA	1,184,572			1,184,572
TIAA CREF Dick IRA	919,083			919,083
TDW Dick Roth	13,701			13,701
TDW Jane IRA		457,008		457,008
TDW Jane Roth		13,501		13,501
Total Qualified Assets	2,117,356	470,509		2,587,865
Lifestyle Assets				
Dick & Jane's Fla Condo			252,500	252,500
Dick & Jane's House			1,060,500	1,060,500
Time Share			12,000	12,000
Total Lifestyle Assets			1,325,000	1,325,000
Life Insurance Cash Value				
Met Life Joint			106,380	106,380
Life Ins. Met Life Jane		2,500		2,500
Life Ins. Met Life Dick	5,000			5,000
Total Life Ins. Cash Value	5,000	2,500	106,380	113,880
Total Assets	3,460,043	1,941,106	2,045,881	7,447,030
Total Net Worth	**3,460,043**	**1,941,106**	**2,045,881**	**7,447,030**

Figure 15

The net worth statement should show all of your assets and your liabilities by ownership, including your home, investment real estate, brokerage accounts, etc. It is important to list how the property is titled, or who owns it. It may be titled individually in your own name, jointly with another person(s), as a tenant in common, or in trust name. These are just some of the ways you can own property.

You also need to list monies inside of tax- deferred vehicles such as IRAs, 401ks, 403bs, pension plans, annuities and insurance products. Add up all of your life insurance, since this may be taxable in your estate. The estate planning scenarios change depending on how your property is titled and the kind of account it is located in.

The three main ways to title your property is in *your name only*, together with another person (several forms of co-ownership) or you could have property *held in a trust* for another person. The way you have your assets titled will effect who will get your assets upon your death.

The Will

It is important for you to have a Will, no matter how your property is titled. Your Will is a document which directs where you want your property to go after your death through the process of probate. You can name specifically who you want to get your home, jewelry, family heirlooms (for example, which niece gets your mother's silverware). You can determine what percentage of your property to go to your brother, cousin, church or favorite charity.

If you don't have a Will, your estate will be distributed by your state's intestate statues and that may not be what you want. For example, some states will divide the property of a childless couple evenly between the surviving spouse and the parents of the deceased spouse and, if the parents weren't alive, half of the money would be given to brothers and sisters of the deceased spouse.

In New York State, assets of a married couple with no children will go to the surviving spouse. Also in New York, if you are not married, have no children and have no Will, your parents will inherit everything. If only one parent is alive, they get everything. If neither parent is alive then your siblings inherit your estate. If they don't survive you and there are no surviving nieces or nephews, then half will go to your next of kin on your mother's side and half to next of kin on your father's side. The heir of last resort will be New York State. I don't think you want N.Y. as your heir, so do some planning.

Executor

In the Will you will name an executor who will be responsible for making sure your final wishes are carried out. The selection of your executor is especially important, since, without children, you may not have anyone else around to be sure your wishes are carried out. If you have ever been an executor of an estate, you know how time-consuming this job can be, so make sure you discuss this appointment with the person prior to giving her/him the assignment.

You should consider the person's age when naming an executor and perhaps add one or two successor executors as backup. Also, consider the fees the executor will get paid and make provisions in your Will for this. On a sizable estate, the fees can really add up (this is why many people with large assets set up trusts, which we will talk about). During the probate process, the court appoints your executor as Personal Representative. To give you an idea of what the personal representative can be paid, I have included the fee schedule below for New York State.

Personal Representative Fees

5%	Commission up to	$100,000
4%	Commission on the next	$200,000
3%	Commission on the next	$700,000

2.5%	Commission on the next	$4 million
2%	Commission anything over	$5 million

A Will's Strengths

A Will determines who will receive your property that transfers through probate. You get to appoint the executor who will carry out your wishes. In the Will you can reduce estate taxes by specifying certain money be left to charities or take advantage of certain tax deductions. A Will gives you flexibility since you can change it anytime before you die. A Will is revocable, and this allows you to make changes to the Will if your personal or financial situation changes or the estate tax law changes.

A Will's Weaknesses

Probating a Will can be expensive. You have attorney fees, fees to the personal representative, and the probate process could drag on for months or years. There also may be problems with the interpretation of a Will drawn up in one state being probated in another state, so it is a good idea if you move to another state to have your Will reviewed.

When your Will is probated, it is a public document that all could view if they want to. Since the Will goes into effect only when you die, it can't help you with incapacitation. For the RINK having a Will may be okay, but you will be better served by having a Revocable Trust. You should also understand that many assets will not pass via your Will. Let me talk about these.

Will Substitutes

You can avoid probate by having your property titled in such a way that the property passes directly to an intended beneficiary. Of course, there are pros and cons to these methods, depending on the total size of your estate. With *Tenants In Common,* if one owner dies, his share must be probated according to his Will. You can title your property *Joint Tenants With Right of Survivorship*

(JTWRS). Each joint tenant has an equal and undivided interest in the property and when you die the other joint owner automatically inherits the entire property.

JTWRS can work well, as long as your estate isn't large enough to worry about estate tax upon the second death, in which case a Bypass Trust would make better sense, this will be discussed later.

You can title real estate, bank accounts and brokerage accounts JTWRS, but you have to be careful if the joint tenant is not your spouse. Say you are on your own and want to avoid the expense of probate so you put your nephew on your bank account as JTWRS. For one thing he could take all of your money out at any time. If he gets sued or divorced (those darn in-laws!), the money in this account could be at risk.

I do not recommend this for the RINK since you are putting your future at risk. I don't care how sweet your nephew is; money can corrupt people, especially if their own personal financial situation takes a turn for the worst. A better way would be to title the bank account *"In Trust For."*

You can title your bank accounts *In Trust For (ITF)* which would offer better protection for you if you are single. This will allow you to avoid probate. Upon your death the bank will pass your account directly to the beneficiary or beneficiaries you name on the application. You are free to do whatever you want with the account and while you are alive, your beneficiaries can't touch the money. When you die they get their share. You maintain control, there is no probate, and you are protected.

Transfer-on-Death (TOD) has been available in many states and now New York State passed legislation to allow TOD registration of stocks, bonds, mutual funds and other investments. This works much like the ITF we discussed above. You can have the account in your name alone, maintain full control over the account, and you are able to designate one or more beneficiaries who will inherit the account upon your death. As with ITF, you can change the beneficiaries at any time without an attorney just by contacting the firm that holds the account and filling out new beneficiary forms. You can even have the account titled jointly as JTWRS with TOD beneficiaries. *Payable On Death (POD)* is similar to TOD and is usually seen on government bonds.

Other assets that can transfer directly are IRAs, pension plans, annuities and life insurance policies. These are what are called *Transfers by contract.* The contract is typically the designation of a beneficiary with the firm holding the assets. You may have most of your total net worth in IRAs that were rolled over from a pension plan. If you have designated a beneficiary none of these pass via your Will, but according to your beneficiary form, with the brokerage firm holding the IRA.

I always ask the client to be sure all of her beneficiary forms are up to date, especially if there has been a death or divorce in her family. She certainly does not want to leave her ex-husband all of her pension money when she thought it would go to her current husband.

A way to have your home pass directly outside of your Will is by having your deed titled with *A Life Estate* interest. This would give you the right to live in your house until you die and then the ownership or *Remainder Interest* would pass to the person you named. You cannot be kicked out of you home while you are alive and the Grantee has no rights to the property until you die, at which time there will be no probate.

Avoiding Probate

We just discussed Will substitutes that will help you avoid probate, which is expensive and may be time consuming. You may say, "Ray, why do I care about probate, I'm married and we have everything titled jointly JTWROS and when the last one of us dies, who cares what happens?" I am assuming if you read this far into the chapter then you do want to minimize estate expenses, reduce estate taxes and be sure your desired beneficiaries receive the maximum amount of your estate as possible with the least amount of headaches.

You might have other issues that need to be dealt with such as what if you become incapacitated, own out-of-state property, have pets, and perhaps the ongoing care of a relative or friend with special needs. All of these issues will have to be dealt with and, for most RINKs a Living Trust is a good answer.

Living Trust

There are many types of trusts that can be created but for our purpose here, which is basic estate planning for the RINK, I will explain the Living Trust (also called the inter vivos trust). The living trust is operative during the grantor's life (usually you) and is considered a *revocable trust* since you have full control and the ability to modify or terminate it during your lifetime.

The living trust document allows you to pass your property directly to your heirs without going through the probate process, which is a major reason most people get living trusts drawn up. For you, there are other features that may be more important, such as the way your affairs will be handled if you become incapacitated.

Many people mistakenly believe a living trust will reduce or avoid estate taxes, but that is not true. There are other trusts, such as *Irrevocable Trusts*, that are created to reduce estate taxes, but I am not discussing those here. The living trust avoids probate and the associated expenses, but doesn't save estate taxes.

Usually, you have an attorney draw up the trust document, you name your self *trustee* and, if you have a spouse, she/he is named co-trustee. If there is no spouse, you can name a relative, trusted friend or advisor who would have control over your affairs if you become incapacitated.

You can also name a *Successor Trustee* who will take over and must follow your wishes in the trust document when you become incapacitated or you die. Once the living trust is created, you now have to re-title all of your assets in the name of the trust, for example: *Jane Doe, Trustee of the Jane Doe Revocable Trust*

Agreement Dated June 1, 2006. This is a big deterrent for many people because it is a lot of trouble; you must re-title your real estate deed, your brokerage and bank accounts, and all of your possessions if you want to keep them out of probate.

A living trust can also be very helpful if you own property in another state, allowing your heirs to avoid the problems of probate in another state. It is also more difficult for disgruntled heirs to protest your final wishes than with the open probate process using a Will. With a living trust your assets can be divided up quickly and dispensed before anyone knows what has gone on, since the trust administration is done privately. You can potentially avoid long, expensive drawn- out lawsuits over your estate and transfer the assets quickly and efficiently to your desired heirs.

Other Living Trust Issues

I believe for many RINKs having a living trust makes a lot of sense, particularly because of the ability to handle incapacity (which I will discuss in more detail in the next chapter). It will cost you more money to have an attorney draw up the living trust than a Will.

You should still have a Will to cover any assets that weren't included in your trust. This type of Will is called a *pour over Will* and can handle assets you didn't title in the name of the trust or you forgot, such as your favorite grandfather's clock.

You should have provisions in your living trust regarding how the trustees will be paid. This needs to be addressed, especially if the trust has provisions in it that will keep it going on for a while. In case you get divorced after the creation of the living trust, you should have it reviewed. It is important to remember that all of the items we discussed under Will Substitutes *will not* be distributed under your living trust either, (for example your IRAs and if you have a house titled jointly JTWRS).

Bypass Trust

A *Bypass Trust,* also called a *Credit Shelter Trust, A B Trust, an exemption equivalent trust or a family trust,* is an irrevocable trust created by one spouse to benefit the other spouse or the heirs when your estate is larger than the current federal estate tax exemption which in 2006 is $2 million.

The purpose of this trust is to reduce estate taxes. This trust does not apply to you if you are single, unless you are a widow/widower who became trustee of a bypass trust upon the death of your spouse. As I said earlier, estate planning can get more complicated the more assets that you have and this strategy is a basic strategy used for married couples in an effort to lower the estate tax bill for their heirs. The bypass trust language is typically built into your Will or living trust.

It is very common for my clients to have the bypass trust language included in their Will, especially if the Will was drawn up when the federal estate tax exemption was only $600,000. While you might think a bypass trust isn't needed because the current federal estate tax exemption is $2 million going up to $3.5 million in 2009 and then in 2010 there is no estate tax, you must remember if the law isn't changed in 2011, the exemption will fall back to only $1 million.

As we discussed, each person upon his death receives a federal exemption in 2006 of $2 million. This means you can leave $2 million to anyone without federal estate taxes. If you are married and leave everything to your spouse, then, of course, there are no estate taxes since, between husband and wife there is no limit on what can be inherited, but you lose the value of the first-to-die's exemption.

Now, upon the death of the second spouse, only one exemption applies. If the law stays as written today and the second death occurs in 2012, then the federal exemption rolls back to just $1 million and the rest is taxed. The purpose of the bypass trust is to take advantage of the value of the first person's exemption upon his death and put the amount of the exemption into the bypass trust where it can grow and eventually upon the second spouse's death pass on to your heirs without estate tax.

Bypass Trust Example

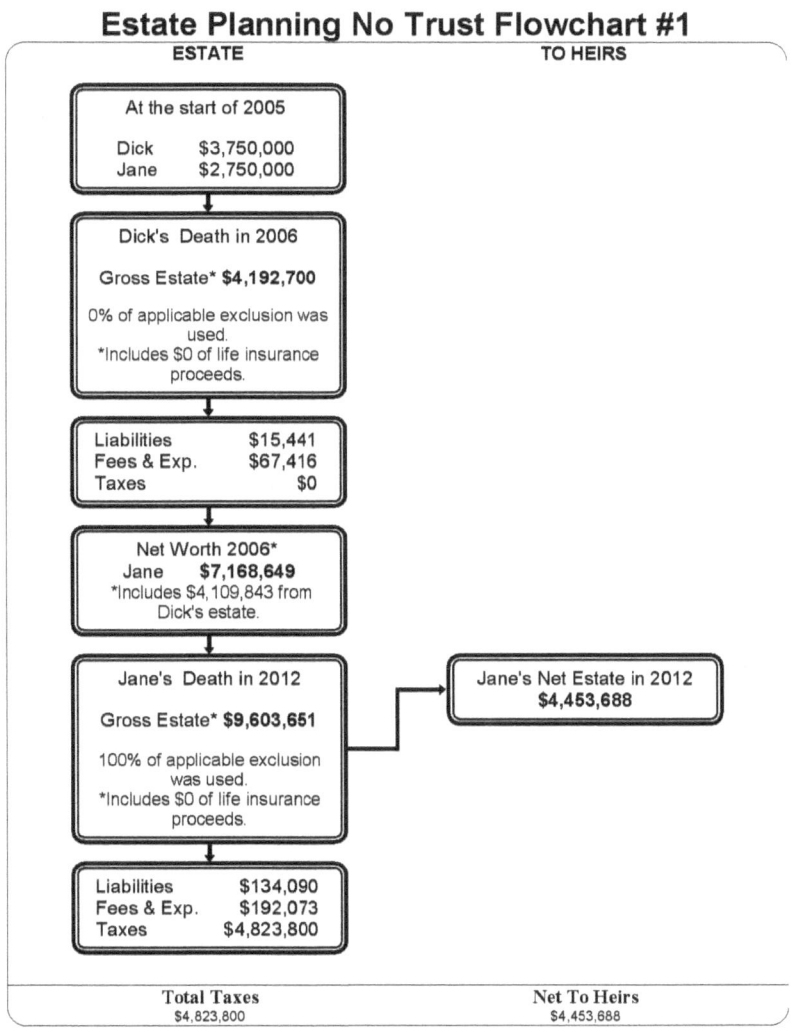

Estate Planning No Trust Flowchart #1

ESTATE	TO HEIRS

At the start of 2005

Dick — $3,750,000
Jane — $2,750,000

Dick's Death in 2006

Gross Estate* **$4,192,700**

0% of applicable exclusion was used.
*Includes $0 of life insurance proceeds.

Liabilities — $15,441
Fees & Exp. — $67,416
Taxes — $0

Net Worth 2006*
Jane **$7,168,649**
*Includes $4,109,843 from Dick's estate.

Jane's Death in 2012

Gross Estate* **$9,603,651**

100% of applicable exclusion was used.
*Includes $0 of life insurance proceeds.

Jane's Net Estate in 2012
$4,453,688

Liabilities — $134,090
Fees & Exp. — $192,073
Taxes — $4,823,800

Total Taxes	Net To Heirs
$4,823,800	$4,453,688

Figure 16

169

To help you get a better idea of the way things would flow with a bypass trust and the taxes saved I have included two scenarios using my planning software to show a couple who in 2005 start off with $6.5 million in their estate, (Figures 16 and 17). This software calls the Bypass Trust a Credit Shelter Trust but it's the same thing.

You see in **flowchart #1**, (Figure 16), the Joneses only have a basic Will and when Dick dies in 2006 all of his money flows to Jane. Then, in 2012 Jane dies when the law drops back to only a $1million exemption for her. While her estate has grown to over $9 million in 2012, approximately half goes to taxes and only half goes to the heir, in this case a loving niece.

In **flowchart #2,** (Figure 17), I added a bypass trust clause to the Joneses' Wills so that when Dick dies in 2006, the trust is funded with approximately $2 million, the then-current exemption amount, and the balance goes to Jane. When Jane dies in 2012 when the exemption is only $1 million, her estate has grown to approximately $6.8 million and the trust has grown to approximately $2.58 million. Upon Jane's death, the entire trust worth $2.58 million passes to the heir without estate tax. The niece will also receive Jane's estate of $3.269 million, net of taxes, for a total of $5.857 million.

By using the bypass trust, the total taxes are approximately $3.4 million and the heir inherits $5.8 million. Just by using the bypass trust in this example approximately $1.4 million more passed to the intended heir than if the couple just had left everything to each other in their Wills.

Note: Since I used actual cash flow-based planning software, this example is more complicated than if I just drew the diagrams. With the software I can simulate a real situation better. Please don't get too distracted by the numbers between the starting value of the estate and the final values, since many calculations are transpiring here which can affect the numbers. Some of those are: A growth rate of 6% for most assets. The New York estate tax being deducted. Income taxes on IRAs. Other expenses and estimated inflation that were in the couple's retirement plan. This would all be shown and explained to you in a detailed meeting.

Estate Planning With Bypass Trust Flowchart #2

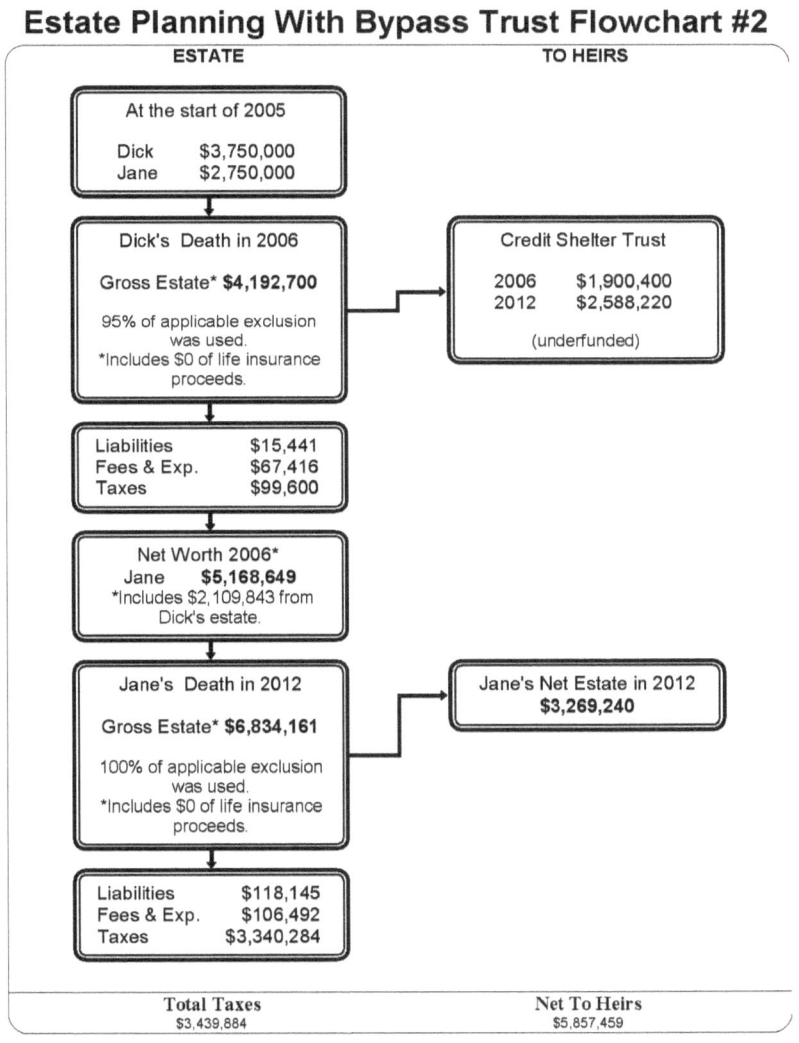

Figure 17

Bypass Trust Details

You can also have this trust language included in a Living Trust document to benefit from both strategies. When the estate planning attorney draws up these documents, he will request that you separate enough assets to match at least the amount needed to fund the bypass trust. If you have everything in joint names (JTWRS), then you will have to retitle your assets either to tenants in common or, better yet, into separate accounts, each under your own names. If you fail to do that you will defeat the purpose of the bypass trust, since it can't be funded properly.

If most of your net worth is tied up in IRAs, this will present other problems and must be discussed with the estate attorney. The bypass trust is irrevocable so, once the money goes into it, the surviving spouse (who is usually co-trustee along with someone else) is not free to do whatever she wants. While irrevocable at death, this trust remains revocable as long as you are competent to change it.

Most trust language allows the surviving spouse access to all trust income and principal as needed for health, maintenance, education and support. In more recent estate plan documents a *disclaimer clause* is put in to allow the surviving spouse the option of funding the trust with the full exemption amount or not. I recommend ensuring this clause is included.

With No Children Do I Need A Bypass Trust?

Remember, a bypass trust is only for married couples and since you don't have children, do you really want to have the surviving spouse's money tied up in an irrevocable trust? Your answer will depend on how much other assets you have, how old you are when your spouse dies, how much you need to live on and, especially, how much you hate paying taxes even when you are dead!

Here are some of the negatives that I see which most attorneys don't spend enough time explaining (or they do but you're overwhelmed with information at the time) and this all has to do with the surviving spouse, since the trust doesn't come into being until the first spouse's death.

When the trust is created upon the first death, you will have to open another brokerage account in the name of the irrevocable trust, say *Dick Jones Family Trust*. You will have to transfer your investments (stocks, bonds, cash) into the new account and that account will have its own EIN number registered with the IRS, (EIN is how the IRS tracks the trust, similar to a social security number). You will now have to file a separate income tax return each year for the trust.

This adds more expense in setting up the trust, funding it, transferring assets and annual tax preparation expense. It also adds a little more complexity to managing your overall portfolio. I think the most important negative is the fact that the surviving spouse does not have totally free access to the funds and must be involved with someone else who is selected as co-trustee to make trust decisions.

Another issue is the increasing federal estate tax exemption amount. For many years, it was only $600,000 and your documents would instruct use of the amount of the then-current exemption to fund the bypass trust. Now, in 2006, the exemption is $2 million. Let's say you have only $3 million in total assets and $500,000 of that is your house. Would you want your surviving spouse to be only left with $500,000 outside of the trust?

If you are 95 and she is 95, well then, maybe, but otherwise I don't think so. If your estate planning documents were drawn up more than a few years ago you should check the language and see how the wording reads as far as funding the trust. You want to be sure you have a disclaimer clause to give the option of not funding the trust upon the first death. If you and your spouse were in your early 60s and your spouse died, unless you have a really large estate, I wouldn't fund the trust.

My advice is: for married couples with significant total assets, it makes sense to have the bypass language built into their estate planning documents as long as the surviving spouse has the ability to not fund it or limit it with a disclaimer clause. If saving taxes is a high priority to you and you want your heirs to have the most possible after-tax money and you are comfortable with the selection of your co-trustee, then fund the trust with as much as you can. Remember, there are a lot of other ways to save taxes, such as gifting while you are alive, using life insurance strategies and leaving money to charity.

The goal throughout this book is to be sure you maintain control and have enough money to allow you to live out the rest of your life in dignity while maintaining the lifestyle you want. So, if anything will put that in jeopardy, I would recommend you not do it.

Giving Away Money While You Are Alive

Starting in 2006, you can give anyone up to $12,000 each year without having to file a gift tax form. If you give more than the $12,000 to someone you must file a gift tax form although no tax will be due until you use up the lifetime gift exemption.

You can give any amount to charity or pay for anyone's education without incurring any taxes. You should be very careful before you give away your money and for the RINK, I like to see you hold on to your money as long as possible to ensure your own needs won't be in jeopardy.

Many times, especially young widows (here when I say young I mean in the early 60s) feel they have more money than they need. They start helping relatives pay their bills, not realizing the amount of money required for themselves over the next 30 plus years.

In general, you need to be selfish and hold onto your money. Your sister, who is always broke (but seems to have a new car every year), or your 45 year-old musician nephew, who refuses to get a "real job", more than likely won't ever be able to repay your generosity and in return help you financially.

My caution to you is to be very careful when you give away your money to be sure you maintain that buffer of a large nest egg you need for your own emergency health care. But while I say you should be selfish for self-preservation reasons, it doesn't mean you have to be a miser altogether.

If you want to help relatives or charities each year, you should do it slowly and, most importantly, while you are monitoring your own financial situation. Here's where all of the retirement planning projections you created become important. Before you do any gifting each year you should update your net worth statement, review your expenses and how your investments have done for the year. If your plan is on track, determine how much you can gift for the year. If your expenses are high for the year and your portfolio didn't do so well, then maybe this year you don't gift or you give less. If you have a trusted advisor, ask him what he thinks you should be doing.

Keep Your Finances Private

In general, it is not a good idea for your friends and family members to know how much money you have since there are some relatives who will hound you to give them some money and cry to you every time their credit card bill arrives.

I see too many "children" in their 40s & 50s who are living way above their means because their income is regularly supplemented by parents or aunts/uncles and they never learn how to stand on their own feet financially. They *expect* their annual gift, sometimes even complaining if it comes late.

Helping someone during an emergency is one thing. Paying for someone's large screen TV while you cut back your own cable TV service to me is ridiculous (but I see it often).

My suggestion is to keep your gift-giving to relatives random, when you can afford it or you think it is needed. This way, gifts aren't expected from you. If you have relatives you want to help, why not take them on vacation and pay for everything, or take them to dinner instead of giving cash? This will help you establish a stronger bond, which is especially important since, as a RINK, you need to have and maintain good, strong life-allies for your ETeam that will be there when you may need assistance.

Chapter Summary

Estate planning strategies are different for you since you don't have children to worry about, but you still want to be sure your assets go to your desired heirs with the least amount of expenses and estate taxes. The current estate tax laws are in flux, so you need to be sure any estate planning you do is with a good estate attorney, preferably one who is also familiar with elder law.

For you, a Will alone may not be the best vehicle because of probate. While you can eliminate most of probate by titling your assets so they flow directly to a beneficiary this raises other issues for the RINK. I think you should consider having a living trust drawn up. In addition to avoiding probate, this makes it much easier for someone to help you if you become incapacitated due to illness.

A bypass or credit shelter trust for married couples can help your heirs save on estate taxes but will complicate the surviving spouse's financial life.

Lastly, be very careful about giving away too much of your money while you are alive. Be sure you have enough so that you are well cared for in your later golden years. Your gifting strategy should be done in conjunction with careful monitoring of your overall financial situation, updating your retirement projections as you go along to ensure you maintain good financial health.

12) Health Care &
Incapacity Planning

Be careful of reading health books. You may die of a misprint.
-Mark Twain

No planning would be complete without planning for your own medical care and possible incapacity. Many of my clients are very dedicated loving sons and daughters of parents who require much assistance in their old age. They dedicate a good part of their own time assisting aged parents and they ask, **"Who will be there for me?"** As a RINK, who *will* take care of you? Or, as one of my RINK clients said to me "I'm not worried about having enough money for the services but who will coordinate all this for me if I can't?"

Who will be there when you need help is the number one concern of all RINKs. Hopefully, you have made a conscious effort to surround yourself with a good support team. Here is where my previous comments about having an established long-term relationship with a trusted financial advisor as head of your $Team comes into play. In this chapter, you will now add a geriatric care manager to possibly lead your ETeam. In addition, your ETeam should include a strong *emotional* network of friends and relatives who are young enough to be able to help you during any health crisis.

Your smart planning will make it easier for them to help you since your documents will have been drawn up ahead of time, detailing your wishes. They will also have access to money to pay for your needs. If you did everything we discussed so far, your finances should be in good shape, so now I want to discuss some other planning strategies that may help you in times of incapacity. Let's start off with some documents that will help with the planning for *your person* (you) since, in the last chapter, we discussed legal documents that took care of *your property*.

Health Care Proxy

The *health care proxy* is a revocable document in which you authorize another person (*your agent*) to make health care decisions for you if you are no longer able to do so for yourself. Some states call this a durable power for health care. Such decisions may include which treatments, such as artificial nutrition, hydration and ventilators, should be provided or withheld and whether you should undergo surgery that may prolong your life but not cure you.

How much authority you wish to give your agent and what particular instructions you wish to have followed is up to you. In addition to a *primary agent* you should appoint an *alternative agent* to assume responsibility if the primary agent, is not available. As with the appointment of an executor in your Will, you should discuss this with the person before appointing him and give him a copy of your document.

To avoid confusion and disagreements you should not appoint more than one agent. Of course you should choose your agent carefully; it should be someone you can count on to follow your wishes, despite other influences. In fact, the person you assign as agent might be someone with a completely different personality than the person you assign in your will or trust to handle your property. In your will or trust, which has more to do with financial matters, you would want someone with a good head for money. In your health care documents you would want someone with a good, compassionate heart.

If you have a Will and not a living trust, it is very important for you to keep a current health care proxy and keep your agent up to date on your wishes. Some attorneys laminate a small copy that you can carry in your wallet. By having a health care agent, you avoid the cost and expense of having the court appoint a *Guardian of your person t*o make decisions for you.

A Living Will

A *living will* is a revocable document that allows you to state in advance what life-sustaining medical measures related to hydration, respiration and nutrition should be taken by a health care provider, if you are incapable of making a health care decision. Another advantage of a living will is that it can help avoid disagreements among family members as to what life-sustaining treatments you desire.

The living will is not a complicated document but you should use the language that is acceptable to the state that you are living in so there will not be questions regarding the validity of your document. If you reside part of the year in two different states, you should check that both states will accept the language in your document or have two documents drawn up, one for each state. This is a simple and inexpensive procedure.

Guardianship Of Your Property

If you didn't make other arrangements, someone must petition the court to have a financial guardian appointed who will be responsible to manage your property and financial affairs if you are legally declared incapacitated. This will require a court hearing to determine your competency, (your ability to manage your financial affairs) which can be embarrassing and degrading.

If you need to have a court appointed guardianship, the proceeding is expensive to set up and expensive to maintain. You will (it comes from your money) have attorney fees to petition the court, court-filing fees, the cost of bond, the court evaluator's fee, the Guardian's fee, and your Guardian's attorney's fees.

While you may have spent a lot of time trying to avoid probate fees, which are paid one time when you die, you also need to think about avoiding the *ongoing costs* if you have to have a court-appointed Guardian. You can avoid having a Guardian appointed by setting up the proper language in your Living Trust to appoint a Successor Trustee for the care of your property upon your incapacity. This is another reason I like Living Trusts along with a Durable Power of Attorney.

Durable Power of Attorney

A *Durable Power of Attorney* (DPOA) is a written document that you execute, authorizing another person to act on your behalf. Unlike a regular power of attorney, the DPOA specifically states that the agent's authority does not cease when you become incapacitated. You can make the power effective immediately or to begin only when you become incapacitated. This would be considered a *springing durable power of attorney*.

In the Durable Power of Attorney the person you grant the authority to is considered the *attorney-in-fact*. This document is relatively less complicated and expensive to create and administer, but some financial institutions may question its authority, especially if it has been some time since its creation.

You also have to determine if you want to limit the agent's authority under the DPOA, since this person could do just about anything you can do with your property, so you must be very careful. Even if you have a living trust with a successor trustee you should have a DPOA, since there may be some things that the successor trustee may not be able to do for you. For example financial decisions outside of the living trust.

When choosing the person to be named as your agent, you must have complete trust in her to put your financial interests ahead of her own.

Living Trusts and Incapacity

If you are acting as trustee of your own living trust and become incapacitated, whomever you have named as your successor trustee will assume the responsibility for managing your assets on your behalf. This way you won't have to worry about who will manage your property and you avoid the expense of guardianship as to the assets in the trust.

If you have assets that are not in your living trust, they will be managed by the person on your DPOA. The person named will manage assets titled by one of the Will substitute methods we spoke about in the last chapter. Your living trust not only avoids probate when you die, it avoids the costs of guardianship if you become incapacitated.

Long-Term Care

Depending on the total amount of your assets you can either decide to self-fund your long-term health care needs, make yourself impoverished and go on *Medicaid,* or purchase a long-term care insurance policy to pay some or all of the expected costs of long term care. In the NYC metropolitan area, a high quality nursing home could cost well over $100,000 a year and it is not uncommon for an extended stay in a nursing home to significantly reduce or totally eliminate a person's total net worth.

It is a misperception if you believe *Medicare* will serve as a primary source of funds for long-term care assistance. Medicare pays for very few long-term care expenses. Medicaid will pay for your long-term care expenses but, in order to qualify, you have to basically impoverish yourself. There are strategies to help shelter your assets to allow you to become eligible for Medicaid but these are beyond the scope of this book, so I would suggest you enlist the services of a qualified Elder law attorney to help in this area, since it is very specialized.

There are many levels of long-term care that are available. Some include home care (either full or part-time), assisted-living facilities, and nursing homes. Most people would prefer to stay in their own home as long as possible. I'm sure you would, also.

Sales pitches from long-term care insurance companies always use the highest costs of a nursing home, but you might be able to hire a live-in aide 24 hours a day for less than $50,000 a year. It all depends on how much help you need and your location, in some areas it will cost less and other areas such as Long Island, N.Y. it can cost up to $70,000 a year. Since you might require different levels of assistance, you need to consider all scenarios, especially the scenario where perhaps you had a minor stroke and needed help for a year, but then no longer needed assistance.

Most financial advisors say that the people who should be paying for long-term care insurance are the children, since it is their inheritance that will be eaten up by the parents' long-term care costs. If we follow that logic, you might conclude, so what? Who cares? I don't have children to worry about, but what if you are married? You buy long-term care insurance to fund quality services while protecting your assets.

LTC Issues For Married Couples

What happens if you deplete all of your assets on your long-term care? You must then ask the question, "Do you want to leave your spouse impoverished?" (I'll assume the answer is NO). You should analyze your financial situation to make a determination if you have enough assets to be sure you can either self-fund the long-term care, take the chance you will just die quickly in your sleep, not incurring any expense, or buy some long term care insurance coverage.

If you are married and have enough assets, and income to fund long-term care, you should probably self-fund. I recently did some planning for a 70 year-old RINK couple who had a net worth of liquid assets over $7 million while spending $150,000 a year. The wife was concerned that she would run out of money with the expense of going into a nursing home.

Using the planning software and simulating a very high $150,000 a year nursing home cost for 5 years, I showed them that they would never run out of money. If they purchased long-term care insurance it would enable them to leave a larger estate. The husband felt he would be leaving a large enough estate and he would rather have the freedom of paying for any kind of health care he desired with his own money and not be restricted by any limitations an insurance company might present.

Their decision was to self-fund and the wife felt much better. It is amazing how sometimes issues that really bother you can be set aside when you see the results of realistic projections. Now, this may not be appropriate for you, since most people don't have such high assets, so each situation has to be looked at individually. But, if you are married, you should consider the insurance and compare its advantages and disadvantages to self-funding your health care.

LTC For The Single RINK

If you are not married, you also have to evaluate the amount of assets and income you have and determine if you should self-fund. The same planning will help you determine this. If you are not married and leaving a large estate is not your priority, then you might decide you don't mind depleting your assets to pay for your own long-term care coverage.

Most studies say the average time spent in a nursing home is four years. It seems to me people are living longer in nursing homes, so you should plan for six years. If you then run out of money, depending on where you live, you will qualify for Medicaid and, in most cases, have exactly the same care. A lot of thought has to go into this decision and, in many cases, the single RINK will decide to buy the long term care insurance just to have peace of mind.

Long Term Care Insurance

While I am not a big fan of paying insurance premiums, long-term care insurance is one type of insurance that, a RINK should consider. For many situations it may make sense to help offset your long-term care costs and give you peace of mind. Long-term care insurance will pay for assistance if you have a chronic disability or illness that leaves you unable to take care of yourself. It may allow you to stay in your own home longer.

People with very few assets and little income need not consider getting a policy since they will be eligible for Medicaid with some planning. If your planning projections allow you to afford $150,000 a year (for each person if you are married) for five years, you may decide to self-fund your care and not get the long-term care insurance.

If you are concerned about leaving a large estate to your heirs or just want the security of knowing you will have extra money available to pay for long-term care, then you should consider the insurance. Also, if your assets are borderline or you are alone and just want the peace of mind, then the insurance makes sense.

You must be sure that you will continue to have the money to pay for the premiums, otherwise, you'll have nothing, but cancelled checks when the time comes to need long term care.

LTC Insurance Details

You should work with your financial advisor, an elder law attorney and someone knowledgeable in long-term care insurance products when trying to determine if and at what age you should take out the policy. You should understand some basic LTC insurance terms.

Individual LTC policies usually pay a set dollar *daily benefit* amount, for example, $150 a day. There are options to have this amount indexed to inflation to keep up with rising health- care costs. The policy may have an elimination period anywhere from 0 to 120 days during which you will have to wait before collecting any benefits, which means you will have to pay out of pocket during that time.

Your LTC policy will also have a defined *benefit period* that will define the maximum length of time your policy will pay. It is usually anywhere between 3 and 5 years, up to a lifetime of coverage. There are *benefit triggers* in each policy; one of the most common definitions concerns *activities of daily living* (ADLs). ADLs may include bathing, toileting, eating, dressing, transferring (ability to move around), and taking medicine.

Usually, if you are unable to perform two or more ADLs, then you will qualify for the policy. There can be other triggers such as a mental impairment caused by Alzheimer's or Parkinson's diseases.

Long Term Care Insurance Costs

The cost of LTC insurance is what prevents most people from buying the policies. If you are in your 50s it is inexpensive but you will be paying for the policy for a very long time with low odds of using it until you are older. When you are older, your odds of using it are greater but you will have a higher annual premium, especially if you develop an illness which the insurance companies don't want to insure.

When investigating LTC insurance, you should work with an agent who represents several companies. This way you are better able to compare features in a true apples to apples comparison. Comparing LTC policies can be very tricky.

Many things will affect the premium you will be quoted such as your age, gender, health, years of coverage, daily amount paid, compounded inflation coverage and length of the elimination period. It is very important to buy your policy from a highly-rated, sound insurance company, which you expect to still be in the LTC insurance business when you need it.

This usually means you may not go with the cheapest premium. Companies that offer very low premiums may end up getting out of the business. Life insurance companies have a long history of experience with life expectancies and have developed sophisticated actuarial models that let them understand their future liability. My concern is that the LTC insurance companies don't have a long enough history of what they can expect to pay out and, therefore, may not be pricing the current premiums realistically.

It doesn't do you any good to pay into a policy every year for 20 years and then the company decides to get out of the LTC business because people are living longer in nursing homes and the LTC insurance company is paying out much more than it originally estimated.

Some things you should look for in a policy are:
* Only one deductible for life.

* That you are covered for preexisting conditions.

* You are not required to first be in a hospital to trigger the benefits.

* You have at least a 5% compounded inflation rider.

* The policy is guaranteed renewable as long as you pay your premiums.

* Your policy should pay for coverage if you receive care in your home from a relative or friend.

Many times, you will get a discount if both husband and wife take out policies. Also, be aware that, depending on your age, part of your long-term care-insurance premium is tax-deductible.

New York State Partnership
In an effort to relieve Medicaid and the state of the escalating burden of long term care coverage, N.Y.S. adopted legislation to establish the NYS Partnership for Long-term Care. If you live in

N.Y.S. and you purchase a partnership policy, you will be covered by the policy for three years and then Medicaid will start paying without any limit on the amount of assets you have. There will still be a Medicaid income test.

This policy makes sense if you don't have a large stream of income coming to you such as a pension, but do have significant assets that you want to leave to your heirs. Sometimes, these policies will cost a little more than other policies, since you must have certain features such as: 3 years coverage, 6 years of home care, and a 5% compounded-annually inflation protection for individuals younger than 79.

While the partnership can only be purchased in NY, it is portable to anywhere in the country, but the Medicaid benefits provided as part of the policy are only available in NY. This policy may make sense for you, so be sure to ask about it when evaluating LTC policies, since many times, the insurance agent will not bring it up. Similar policies are available in Indiana, Connecticut and California. Currently, there is an effort to make this type of policy available nationwide.

Are Geriatric Care Managers Your Answer?

I believe the growing field of professional *geriatric care managers* will increasingly play a vital role in our future health care and support. As a RINK, most of us will have to pay for a larger part of our services than someone with caring children.

A good geriatric care manager will be the answer when we are alone and don't have a caring relative or friend with the time or inclination to help. Besides, do you want to bother friends or relatives anyway?

The purpose of this book is for you to manage your investments intelligently and do your planning conservatively so you will have enough assets to be able to pay for services to maintain your quality of life and independence in retirement. Finding and hiring a good quality geriatric care manager can play a vital role in your future. What does a geriatric care manager do and how can they help you?

According to the National Association of Professional Geriatric Care Managers, Inc., a **geriatric care manager** is a health and human services professional, such as a gerontologist, nurse, social worker, or psychologist, with a specialized focus on issues related to aging and elder care. **Geriatric care managers** work privately with older adults and their families to create a plan of care that meets the needs of the older adult. They will meet with you to help you understand your needs and to learn what resources and options are available to meet those needs.

Most geriatric care managers are committed to maximizing the independence and autonomy of elders. They can act in many capacities, depending on your needs, and they have a very wide range of services that can be performed. When necessary, they can coordinate with elder law attorneys, health insurance professionals, realtors and other professionals to ensure all your needs are considered. Even some financial advisors are getting more involved with geriatric care managers to help their clients.

Some of their services include: assessing your condition; doing ongoing case management; orchestrating shopping; errands and transportation; arranging for and monitoring home health aids; arranging for placement in social and medical day programs; assessing home safety and arranging for necessary repairs; preparing Medicaid applications if needed; and providing help with evaluating and placement in assisted living facilities, nursing homes; and assisting with just about anything you would need help with.

Finding A Geriatric Care Manager

People calling themselves care managers have many different backgrounds. Very few states have licensing for these professionals; however, many are licensed in their state in other fields. In addition, there is an alphabet soup of designations and credentials that professionals from different fields have who also become geriatric care managers.

Geriatric care managers bring more to their practice than an expertise in geriatrics. They bring knowledge of aging issues that allow them and their staff to focus on your specific problems and issues. At the same time, they bring an experience of working with resources in your community that can be valuable; they already have contacts with other professionals who can help you.

They can assist with a variety of the real-life problems, health and otherwise, that emerge as you age. They also know what tools are available to address your needs. A good geriatric care manager is skilled at coordinating your needs because she is tied into your local system of social workers, nurses, psychologists, elder law attorneys/advocates, and other elder-care professionals who may be of assistance to you.

To locate someone in your area try contacting the National Association of Professional Geriatric Care Managers, Inc. <u>www.caremanager.org</u>

Questions To Ask the Care Manager

Here are some questions you should ask when looking for a geriatric care manager:

* ⋆ Are you certified as a care manager?

* ⋆ What other professional licenses or certifications do you hold?

* ⋆ How long have you been providing care management services?

* ⋆ What is your list of services?

* ⋆ What are the hours I can contact you?

* ⋆ Are you available for emergencies, and do you have a backup?

* ⋆ Does your company also provide home care services?

* Does your company provide other health care services such as, psychotherapy or nursing?

* How will you communicate information to me?

* Can you provide me with references of others in my situation?

* Is there a fee for the initial consultation?

* How do you charge, and how much for each service?

Geriatric Care Manager Fees

Of course we are always concerned about fees, but with geriatric care managers, each case is so unique, depending on what services are provided that you or a friend or an advocate will have to interview several, and get written estimates of their fees. There are many different ways of charging fees and each care manager will choose to work differently.

You will also want to know how often she bills. Some care managers bill weekly, some bill monthly, and some bill upon completion of work. Ask about this at your initial meeting and ask to have the fee schedule put in writing, so there will be no surprises. If you don't understand, ask again. Better yet, have someone else with you or have your financial advisor or attorney review the agreement before you sign.

In addition to fees, most care managers will charge you for their expenses. Out-of-pocket expenses may include charges for mileage, care-giving supplies, long-distance telephone calls, and other such costs. Find out if there will be any other incidental costs.

Be sure to discuss and make sure you have all questions answered before proceeding with an agreement for services. You should expect to be given a written agreement, including fees, before you begin starting services.

Chapter Summary

In this chapter we discussed the necessary legal documents to use to plan for *your person* in addition to the estate-planning documents we discussed previously for the planning of *your property.*

Some of these documents include the Living Will, Health Care Proxy, Durable Power of Attorney, and Living Trust. We also discussed how you should prepare these documents ahead of time to avoid the loss of control, expense and embarrassment of having a court-appointed Guardian and to ensure that your wishes are carried out more easily.

To handle your long term care needs you have to decide whether you should self-fund your long term care needs, make yourself impoverished and go on Medicaid, or purchase a long-term care insurance policy. A good review of your financial situation and your retirement projections should help determine if you should self-fund.

If you decide on long-term care insurance, it is important to work with someone who can show you several different policies from different insurance companies and, if you live in NYS, you should investigate the NY Partnership Program.

You should also be aware that a good geriatric care manager can offer you a wide variety of services and may be one of your best allies as you get older and need some help. Working with the care manager and a good financial advisor should help you maintain your independence and dignity during your retirement.

13) Planning For Your Pet

It wasn't raining when Noah built the ark.
                                              -Howard Ruff

A concern you might have is, what will happen to my pets if I die and who will take care of them? If you are advanced in age and/or suffer from a chronic illness and you have a fairly young pet the odds are your pet may outlive you. Also, if you have an extended stay in the hospital, do you want to worry about who is caring for your pet? This is the reason people leave money in their Wills for the care of their pets or why you would have a *pet trust* created.

Many people, especially RINKs, are very attached to their pets, more in the later years of retirement. Sometimes, your pet helps you get through the long days when there is no one else around for company. Many studies have shown that having a pet actually enhances both your mental and physical health in retirement, especially if you have a life-threatening illness. For all of these reasons and more, you may want to provide for your pet's care by having language put in your Will or by having a pet trust drawn up and providing for its funding.

This way, if you're not confident that someone will take care of your pet, you will have the peace of mind knowing, if something happened to you, your pet will be well taken-care of. Unfortunately, too often the heirs and beneficiaries whom you appointed in your estate planning may not be the best people to take care of your pet.

You should never leave money directly to a pet in a Will or a trust. While you may consider your pet to be a beloved member of your family, U.S. laws generally regard pets as property. As property, pets cannot directly receive money or property as human beneficiaries can. Instead, you can appoint a person to serve as the *guardian* of your pet in your Will. Although this arrangement lacks the formality of an official pet trust, you can still leave the guardian a certain amount of money to take care of your pets.

The Pet Trust

Under a pet trust, the caretaker, or human beneficiary, will be supervised by the *trustee* of the trust. A trustee is someone you select to administer your money or property to your pet's caretaker. The trustee handles the financial matters and you may designate to the trustee the responsibility of monitoring the health and welfare of your pet by overseeing the caretaker to ensure the proper care is being given.

In a pet trust you name a human *beneficiary* to act as a *caretaker* for your pet (Some attorneys like to give the trustee the ability to determine who the caretaker of your pet will be). Be sure to include the address and contact information of all those named in the trust. The choice of beneficiary is one of the most important you will make in setting up a pet trust, since the beneficiary will handle all future daily care for your pet. It's a good idea to designate a *second beneficiary*, in the event that the primary beneficiary is unable or unwilling to assume responsibility for the pet. In addition, you need to name a *successor beneficiary*, either a person or charity that will receive whatever remains in the trust after your pet dies.

The trust should state your wishes regarding what should happen with your pet at the time of your death. In addition, you should take the time to specify the name, breed, and genetic information as well as listing distinguishing markings of your pet. Identifying your pet clearly will prevent fraud. Have a photo ID or for a show dog possibly paw prints. There have been a good number of cases where a caretaker has continued collecting on the trust once the pet died by simply purchasing a new animal that looked like the first pet.

In order to create a viable trust, you must designate or set aside a certain amount of money that will be used for the care for your pet. Consider how much you currently spend on your pet's care and medical expenses to decide what standard of care you wish to provide for financially. If you will use a service to care for your pet consult with them about how much they would require. This decision may also depend on your pet's life expectancy and even the size of your estate. To give you some idea, the average amount left to pets is about $25,000, says Lawyers Weekly USA, a trade journal that has surveyed pet lawyers. In New York State a pet trust can't last more that 21 years, which may present a problem for some pets such as parrots.

Trust Instructions

In the trust you should provide instruction on as many details as you can, sometimes this is done with a separate letter of instructions to the trustee. The names of the favorite foods, sleeping arrangements, and any special needs your pet may have. This should be detailed so that the caretaker you have selected can easily manage the transition. You should also include instructions on the final disposition of your pet's body. By providing specific instructions, you can help ensure that your pet will be cared for according to your wishes for the rest of its lifetime.

How specific should you get in describing your pet's care and maintenance? You know your pet's habits and preferences better than anyone, so be as detailed as possible to insure that your pet gets the care to which he is accustomed. In addition to items we already mentioned, you probably want to include such details as exercise routines (such as walks in the park): who your vet is; how often your pet visits the vet; vet maintenance routines: and any chronic health conditions for which your pet must take medication or receive regular health treatment.

Provide As Much Pet Information as Possible

After seeing on TV what happened to all the abandoned pets following hurricane Katrina in New Orleans, many pet owners want to know what can be done to help their pet if something should happen to them. One idea is that you can carry a pet information card on you at all times which contains information about your pet such as its name, type of animal, location where housed, and special care instructions along with the information necessary to contact someone who can obtain access to your pet.

If you are injured or killed, emergency personnel will recognize that an animal is relying on your return for care and may notify the named person or take other steps to locate and provide for your pet. The card may assure that your pet survives to the time when your plans for the pet's long-term care takes effect, as detailed in your will or pet trust.

Also consider preparing another document containing the same information as on the pet information card and perhaps additional details as well. You should keep this document in the same location where you keep your other estate planning documents. You can keep this updated and provide even more information than you would write directly into a pet trust or in case you don't create a pet trust.

You should consider providing signs in your home to alert any police, firefighters or emergency personnel who may have to come to your home that a pet also lives there. This way in case you are incapacitated, the emergency personnel will be alert to look for someone to care for your pet.

Other Pet Trust Information

A trust is usually taxed on any income generated in the trust. It's important to note that the laws concerning pet trusts can differ from state to state. There is specific legal language required to establish an enforceable trust for the care of a pet. The following states have adopted some version of the Uniform Probate Code's law on animal trusts: Alaska, Arizona, Arkansas, California, Colorado, District of Columbia, Florida, Idaho, Illinois, Iowa, Kansas, Maine, Michigan, Missouri, Montana, Nebraska, Nevada, New Hampshire, New Jersey, New Mexico, New York, North Carolina, Oregon, Rhode Island, Tennessee, Texas, Utah, Washington and Wyoming.

Retire Your Pet To The Hamptons!

Why not plan for your beloved pet to spend its retirement years in the Hamptons? Well you certainly can. When I heard about Bide-A-Wee's Golden Years Retirement Home located in Westhampton on Long Island, N.Y. the write up was so inviting I wanted to sign myself up (my wife always wanted a place in the Hamptons!).

Bide-A-Wee is a non-profit humane organization located in the New York metro area (I'm sure there are similar organizations in most areas of the country). Here is a description of the Golden Years Retirement Home, directly from their website.

"The Golden Years Retirement Home offers dormitory-style accommodations that allow for socialization and privacy, as the residents choose. The full-time staff and volunteers are committed to providing the cats and dogs with quality playtime and exercise along with required daily care." Wouldn't you be relieved if you arranged for your pet to be taken care of in a home like this if something should happen to you?

A Bide-A-Wee Manager told me, "Far too often I get phone calls from mourning family members that don't know what to do with Grandma's beloved pooch or kitty. While I can help these people, nothing replaces Grandma's wishes explicitly expressed in a Will or other testamentary document."

Admission is primarily limited to companion animals whose guardians are no longer able to care for them due to sickness or death. They request payment of $15,000 per animal, generally paid from the animal guardian's estate. When dealing with an estate, Bide-A-Wee understands that probating a Will can be a lengthy process, distribution of funds may take months, even years, so Bide-A-Wee admits the animals into the home before payment is received as long as Bide-A-Wee is mentioned in the decedent's Will or planning document.

I mention Bide-A-Wee since I believe it is an example of a fine organization that has experience working with pet planning. Other non profit and for profit pet long term care facilities are located across the country, all you need to do is search on the internet.

You can reach Bide-A-Wee at **(212) 532-6395 or** www.bideawee. org

Chapter Summary

As with all of your planning, you should also plan for the long-term care of your pet in case something happens to you. By specifically providing instructions and leaving money, you can be sure your pet will have adequate care. You can leave instructions in your will or you can create a pet trust whose sole purpose would be to provide for your pet.

In your documents you should provide specific information regarding your pet's care, type of food, medical problems, name of vet, etc. You should also name the beneficiary who will be caretaker for your pet as well as a secondary beneficiary. In addition, you should name a successor beneficiary who will receive the balance of any money left after your pet dies. This could be a charity.

You may also want to carry a card on you and leave a document in your home for emergency workers to be aware that if something happens to you, there is a pet to be taken care of. If you love your pets, ensure you plan for their care.

Additional Information

I have included the wording below for the New York statutes for pet trusts just to give you an idea of the law.

N.Y. Est. Powers & Trusts Law § 7-8.1 effective 1996
§ 7-8.1. Honorary trusts for pets

(a) A trust for the care of a designated domestic or pet animal is valid. The intended use of the principal or income may be enforced by an individual designated for that purpose in the trust instrument or, if none, by an individual appointed by a court upon application to it by an individual, or by a trustee. Such trust shall terminate when no living animal is covered by the trust, or at the end of twenty-one years, whichever occurs earlier.

(b) Except as expressly provided otherwise in the trust instrument, no portion of the principal or income may be converted to the use of the trustee or to any use other than for the benefit of a covered animal.

(b) Upon termination, the trustee shall transfer the unexpended trust property as directed in the trust instrument or, if there are no such directions in the trust instrument, the property shall pass to the estate of the grantor.

(c) A court may reduce the amount of the property transferred if it determines that amount substantially exceeds the amount required for the intended use. The amount of the reduction, if any, passes as unexpended trust property pursuant to paragraph (c) of this section.

(d) If no trustee is designated or no designated trustee is willing or able to serve, a court shall appoint a trustee and may make such other orders and determinations as are advisable to carry out the intent of the transferor and the purpose of this section

[renumbered from former § 7-6.1 in 2003]

Postscript

I hope the material in this book contributes to your prosperity, and helps you enjoy a long, healthy, and happy retirement.

It is easy just to read a book, absorb new ideas, and never get around to doing anything about it. In the current environment where defined benefit pensions are being eliminated and the viability of Social Security is questionable; it is incumbent upon you to manage your assets wisely. You should recognize the fact that most people need some form of help with planning and investments.

Our firm works with clients from all parts of the country, some we have never met in person. Using technology we have been able to provide a very valuable service to retirees, helping to optimize their wealth and quality of life. To better enable us to help our RINK clients, we created the unique retirement and investment management process we call, the **RINKs Planning Strategy.** Most of the material I wrote about in this book is from this strategy; let me list 10 steps in the strategy.

RINKs Planning Strategy
1) Understand client's current financial, health, and emotional situation.
2) Understand client's immediate needs and long term objectives.

3) Gather all pertinent financial documentation and emergency contacts.
4) Analyze budget, cash flow, and net worth.
5) Create retirement projections and review together.
6) Review estate, health, and charitable planning needs.
7) Review investments, determine needs, and risk tolerance.
8) Create a risk controlled globally diversified investment strategy.
9) Implement investment strategy with continuous management.
10) Monitor and adjust the investment strategy to ensure it continues to meet the retirement projections.

If you would like more information on retirement planning or the RINKs Planning Strategy, please visit our website: www.raymignone.com

Index

About The Author

Raymond D. Mignone is President of Ray Mignone & Co., Inc. an independent Fee-Only financial planning and investment management firm located in Little Neck, N.Y. specializing in working with individuals transitioning into retirement, physicians, and upper middle class retirees.

He became a CERTIFIED FINANCIAL PLANNER™ practitioner in 1989 and since has worked with many individuals and professionals creating financial plans and successfully managing investment portfolios.

Mignone is currently President of the Long Island chapter of the Financial Planning Association (FPA), and the V.P. of Ethics for the past 5 years. He is a member of the National Association of Personal Financial Advisors (NAPFA) and was named "One of the Best 150 Advisors for Doctors", by Medical Economics magazine, also named as one of the nations top professional advisors in J.K. Lasser's book, "New Rules For Estate and Tax Planning".

He has appeared on both Queens and Long Island public television and is frequently sought out by the media to contribute to articles in publications including, The Wall Street Journal, N.Y. Times, Barrons, Newsday, Kiplingers Retirement Guide, N.Y. Daily News, N.Y. Post, Business Week, CNNmoney, Associated Press, Reuters and many others. For the past 6 years he has written a retirement planning and investment column for the Queens Times/Ledger chain of newspapers. Mignone has been a featured speaker and lecturer at numerous financial conferences, investment clubs, and community and business groups.

Prior to getting his CFP® Mignone spent over 10 years working for the International Business Machine Corp. in various management positions, before that he served 4 years in the U.S. Air Force. He received his Bachelor of Science Degree from Adelphi University. Ray and his wife Paula reside in New York and look forward to eventually being RINKs.

If you would like to find out more about Ray Mignone's firm or to have him speak to your group or organization, you can contact him via email. info@raymignone.com

For more information about his unique service for RINKs, the "RINKs Planning Strategy" visit his website at www.raymignone. com